# BBC goodfood

## BEST-EVER CURRIES

Editor **Sarah Cook**

# Contents

# Introduction

Versatile and flavoursome, the popularity of curries has grown and grown, and they're now a favourite among our readers, who are always asking the Good Food team for more. So, what's our solution? Pick our favourites and put them all into one useful little book, and this revised and updated edition has all the best recipes for every occasion.

From quick supper ideas using a few store-cupboard ingredients to elaborate dishes cooked from scratch that are perfect for impressing friends, we've included Thai, Indian and Caribbean varieties, plus some low-fat and healthy recipes for those watching their waistline. But this book isn't just about the main event; we've also included some delicious side dishes and desserts, so you'll have everything you need. Plus each one has been triple-tested, so you know they will work for you.

Most of these recipes feed a family of four, but curries are easily doubled if you're feeding a crowd and taste even better second time around if there are only two of you, as the flavours develop beautifully. Work your way through the chapters, cooking up classics and experimenting with some of the more unusual ideas. So bin the takeaway menu, grab those spices and get cooking!

*Sarah*

Sarah Cook
BBC Good Food Magazine

# Notes &
# Conversion Tables

. . . . . . . . . . . . . . . . . . . . .

## NOTES ON THE RECIPES
- Eggs are large in the UK and Australia and extra large in America unless stated.
- Wash fresh produce before preparation.
- Recipes contain nutritional analyses for 'sugar', which means the total sugar content including all natural sugars in the ingredients, unless otherwise stated.

## OVEN TEMPERATURES

| GAS | °C | °C FAN | °F | OVEN TEMP. |
|---|---|---|---|---|
| ¼ | 110 | 90 | 225 | Very cool |
| ½ | 120 | 100 | 250 | Very cool |
| 1 | 140 | 120 | 275 | Cool or slow |
| 2 | 150 | 130 | 300 | Cool or slow |
| 3 | 160 | 140 | 325 | Warm |
| 4 | 180 | 160 | 350 | Moderate |
| 5 | 190 | 170 | 375 | Moderately hot |
| 6 | 200 | 180 | 400 | Fairly hot |
| 7 | 220 | 200 | 425 | Hot |
| 8 | 230 | 210 | 450 | Very hot |
| 9 | 240 | 220 | 475 | Very hot |

## APPROXIMATE WEIGHT CONVERSIONS
- All the recipes in this book list both imperial and metric measurements. Conversions are approximate and have been rounded up or down. Follow one set of measurements only; do not mix the two.
- Cup measurements, which are used in Australia and America, have not been listed here as they vary from ingredient to ingredient. Kitchen scales should be used to measure dry/solid ingredients.

*Good Food* is concerned about sustainable sourcing and animal welfare. Where possible, humanely reared meats, sustainably caught fish (see fishonline.org for further information from the Marine Conservation Society) and free-range chickens and eggs are used when recipes are originally tested.

## SPOON MEASURES

Spoon measurements are level unless otherwise specified.

- 1 teaspoon (tsp) = 5ml
- 1 tablespoon (tbsp) = 15ml
- 1 Australian tablespoon = 20ml (cooks in Australia should measure 3 teaspoons where 1 tablespoon is specified in a recipe)

## APPROXIMATE LIQUID CONVERSIONS

| METRIC | IMPERIAL | AUS | US |
|--------|----------|-----|-----|
| 50ml | 2fl oz | ¼ cup | ¼ cup |
| 125ml | 4fl oz | ½ cup | ½ cup |
| 175ml | 6fl oz | ¾ cup | ¾ cup |
| 225ml | 8fl oz | 1 cup | 1 cup |
| 300ml | 10fl oz/½ pint | ½ pint | 1¼ cups |
| 450ml | 16fl oz | 2 cups | 2 cups/1 pint |
| 600ml | 20fl oz/1 pint | 1 pint | 2½ cups |
| 1 litre | 35fl oz/1¾ pints | 1¾ pints | 1 quart |

# Thai red salmon curry

· · · · · · · · · · · · · · · · · · · · ·

Thai curry paste can vary in temperature from fairly mild to very hot. If you're using an authentic Thai label, add 1 teaspoon at first, then more to taste.

🕐 15 minutes    🍽 4

- 1 tsp vegetable or sunflower oil
- 1 tbsp Thai red curry paste
- 1 onion, sliced
- 250ml/9fl oz reduced-fat coconut milk
- 2 x 250g skinless salmon fillets, cut into chunks
- 200g/8oz trimmed green beans
- a few coriander leaves, to garnish
- steamed or boiled rice, to serve

1 Heat the oil in a large pan, then add the curry paste. Stir in the onion and cook for about 5 minutes until softened. Pour in the coconut milk and bring to the boil.

2 Reduce to a simmer, then add the salmon chunks and beans. Leave to simmer gently for 5 minutes until the fish flakes easily and the beans are tender. Scatter with the coriander and serve with rice.

· · · · · · · · · · · · · · · · · · · · ·
*PER SERVING 326 kcal, protein 27g, carbs 5g, fat 22g, sat fat 9g, fibre 2g, sugar 4g, salt 0.46g*

# Oven-baked Thai chicken rice

This dish is like a Thai version of a pilaf; try adding baby sweetcorn when in season for extra crunch.

🕐 30 minutes    🍴 4

- 1 tbsp vegetable oil
- 1 onion, chopped
- 400g pack mini chicken fillets
- 4 tbsp Thai green curry paste
- 250g/9oz basmati and wild rice mix, rinsed
- 2 red peppers, deseeded and cut into wedges
- finely grated zest and juice 1 lime
- 400ml can reduced-fat coconut milk
- handful coriander leaves, to garnish

1 Heat oven to 200C/180C fan/gas 6. Heat the oil in a shallow ovenproof casserole dish over a medium heat. Tip in the onion and soften for 5 minutes. Increase the heat, add the chicken and curry paste, and cook for 2 minutes, stirring to coat.

2 Tip in the rice and peppers, then stir in the lime zest and juice, coconut milk and 250ml/8fl oz boiling water. Bring to the boil, then pop the lid on and bake in the oven for 20 minutes until the rice is fluffy. Scatter with coriander before serving.

*PER SERVING 510 kcals, protein 32g, carbs 59g, fat 18g, sat fat 10g, fibre 2g, sugar 8g, salt 1.02g*

# Chicken & chickpea curry

If you don't like chickpeas, simply swap them for a can of red lentils, which will also help the sauce thicken nicely.

 30 minutes  4

- 4 tbsp vegetable oil
- 400g/14oz boneless skinless chicken breasts, cut into chunks
- 2 onions, sliced
- 2 tbsp medium curry powder
- 425ml/¾ pint chicken stock
- 410g can chickpeas, drained and rinsed
- 2 tbsp natural yogurt
- boiled rice, to serve

1 Heat 2 tablespoons of the oil in a frying pan, then add the chicken chunks and fry for a few minutes to brown, stirring. Remove the chicken to a plate, tip half the onions into the pan and cook for 5 minutes until softened. Return the chicken to the pan with the curry powder and stir for a couple of minutes until the chicken and onions are coated in the spice.

2 Pour in the stock and chickpeas, bring to the boil then simmer, covered, for 10 minutes until the chicken is almost cooked through.

3 Meanwhile, heat the remaining oil in a separate pan, add the rest of the onions and fry over a high heat for 5 minutes until crisp and brown. Drain on kitchen paper.

4 Stir the yogurt into the curry and bubble for a few minutes, uncovered. Serve with rice, scattered with the crispy onions.

*PER SERVING 341 kcals, protein 31g, carbs 20g, fat 16g, sat fat 2g, fibre 6g, sugar 4g, salt 1.47g*

# Sweet & spicy fish

If you're watching your calorie intake, make a lighter version by using half the amount of coconut milk topped up with 200ml/7fl oz vegetable or chicken stock.

🕐 25 minutes    🍽 4

- 3 tbsp medium curry paste
- 1 large onion, halved and sliced
- 1 red pepper, deseeded and thickly sliced
- small bunch coriander, leaves and stems separated and roughly chopped
- 400ml can reduced-fat coconut milk
- large handful dried mango pieces, chopped
- 700g/1lb 9oz firm skinless white fish fillets, cut into large chunks
- naan bread, to serve

1 Heat the curry paste in a large pan and fry the onion for 3 minutes until starting to soften. Stir in the sliced pepper and coriander stems, and cook for another 2 minutes. Pour in the coconut milk, tip in the mango pieces and bring to the boil. Season to taste, turn down the heat and simmer for 5 minutes until slightly thickened.

2 Add the fish and cook for 3–5 minutes or until it flakes easily. Sprinkle the coriander leaves over the curry just before serving with warmed naan bread.

*PER SERVING 332 kcals, protein 35g, carbs 18g, fat 14g, sat fat 9g, fibre 2g, sugar none, salt 1g*

# Chickpea curry roll-ups

· · · · · · · · · · · · · · · · · · · · ·

To make a tasty yogurt sauce, mix 200g/8oz low-fat natural yogurt with 1 teaspoon turmeric powder and 2 tablespoons chopped mint leaves.

🕐 20 minutes    🍽 4

- 1 tbsp olive oil
- 2 onions, sliced
- thumb-sized knob ginger, grated
- 1 tbsp garam masala
- 400g can cherry tomatoes
- 410g can chickpeas, drained and rinsed
- 500g bag spinach leaves
- 8 chapattis
- natural yogurt, to serve

1 Heat the oil in a large frying pan, then gently cook the onions and ginger for 5 minutes until beginning to soften. Stir in the spice, cook for 1 minute, then add the tomatoes and chickpeas. Fill the tomato can one-third full with water, tip this in too, then bubble for 5 minutes until the sauce has thickened a little. Stir in three-quarters of the spinach leaves, a handful at a time, then warm through for a few minutes.

2 Heat the chapattis in the microwave or oven according to the pack instructions. Serve the curry spooned over the warm chapattis, with the remaining spinach and a dollop of yogurt, if you like.

· · · · · · · · · · · · · · · · · · · · · · · · · ·
*PER SERVING 424 kcals, protein 19g, carbs 64g, fat 12g, sat fat 2g, fibre 7g, sugar 14g, salt 1.81g*

# Turkey & potato curry

This is a great recipe for using up leftovers. Make it with your Christmas turkey or a roast chicken from Sunday lunch.

🕐 20 minutes   🥧 4

- 1 tbsp sunflower oil
- 1 large onion, thickly sliced
- 1 green pepper, deseeded and chopped
- 2 tbsp curry paste
- 2 garlic cloves, crushed
- 400g can chopped tomatoes
- 300g/10oz cooked turkey, diced
- 300g/10oz leftover cooked potatoes (either boiled or roast), diced
- 2 tbsp mango chutney
- small pack coriander, roughly chopped
- boiled rice or warmed naan bread, to serve

1 Heat the oil in a large pan over a high heat. Cook the onion and pepper for 3–4 minutes until starting to soften and brown slightly. Stir in the curry paste and garlic, then cook for another 1–2 minutes. Add the chopped tomatoes and 150ml/¼ pint water. Bring to the boil and bubble for 5 minutes.

2 Turn the heat down, stir in the turkey and potatoes, and cook for another 2–3 minutes, then season and add the mango chutney. Scatter with coriander and serve with boiled rice or warmed naan.

# Aromatic prawn & cashew curry

Garam masala provides the base spice for this creamy fish curry, which is also flavoured with nuts, green chilli and a tomato-yogurt sauce.

🕐 1 hour 10 minutes   🥧 4

- 1 onion, chopped
- thumb-size knob ginger, peeled and roughly chopped
- 4 garlic cloves, peeled
- 2 green chillies, deseeded
- small bunch coriander, stalks roughly chopped, leaves picked
- 1 tbsp butter or ghee
- 1 tbsp sunflower oil
- 2 tbsp garam masala
- 150g bag unsalted cashew nuts
- 400g can chopped tomatoes
- 400ml/14fl oz chicken stock
- 400g/14oz raw peeled king prawns
- 150ml pot natural yogurt
- 50ml/2fl oz double cream
- rice and naan bread, to serve

1 Put the onion, ginger, garlic, chillies and coriander stalks in a small food processor, or pestle and mortar, and mix to a paste. Meanwhile, heat the butter or ghee and oil in a large pan. Add the paste to the pan and stir-fry for 5 minutes to soften. Add the garam masala and cook for a further 2 minutes until aromatic.

2 Meanwhile, toast the cashew nuts in a small pan until golden. Tip half into a clean food processor and blend until finely ground reserving the remaining cashews.

3 Add the blended cashews, the tomatoes and chicken stock to the pan. Season and bring to a boil, then lower the heat and simmer, covered with a lid, for 45 minutes. Add the prawns and cook for a further 2–3 minutes until they turn pink, then add the yogurt and double cream, and stir well. Scatter with the coriander leaves and the remaining cashew nuts, and serve with boiled rice and warmed naan bread.

*PER SERVING 507 kcals, protein 32g, carbs 18g, fat 34g, sat fat 12g, fibre 4g, sugar 9g, salt 1g*

# Pea & new potato curry

A low-fat and low-calorie vegetable curry that is made with Madras spice and yogurt.

🕐 1 hour 25 minutes   🍽 4

- 1 tbsp vegetable oil
- 2 onions, sliced
- 3 red chillies, deseeded and finely sliced
- thumb-sized knob ginger, roughly chopped
- 2 tsp cumin seeds
- 1 tsp Madras curry powder
- ½ tsp turmeric powder
- 750g/1lb 10oz new potatoes, halved
- juice 1 lime
- small bunch coriander, stalks and leaves finely chopped
- 200–300ml/½ pint vegetable stock
- 300g/10oz podded fresh peas (or use frozen)
- 500ml pot natural yogurt
- lime wedges, to squeeze over
- warmed naan bread, to serve

1 Heat the oil in a large deep frying pan. Add the onions and cook over a low heat for 10–15 minutes until soft. Throw in the chillies, ginger and spices, and cook for a few minutes. Stir in the potatoes and lime juice, coating in the spice mix.

2 Add the coriander stalks and stock to the pan. Simmer slowly for 35–40 minutes until the potatoes are soft and the sauce has reduced. Stir through the peas and cook for another 5 minutes. Add the yogurt, sprinkle over the coriander leaves and serve with lime wedges and warm naan bread.

*PER SERVING 336 kcals, protein 16g, carbs 50g, fat 8g, sat fat 3g, fibre 9g, sugar 18g, salt 0.5g*

# No-fry Thai curry

A perfect after-work curry for two – 5 minutes chopping then 10 minutes in the pan.

 15 minutes  🍽 2

- 2 rounded tbsp Thai green curry paste
- 400ml can coconut milk
- 2 skinless chicken breast fillets, very thinly sliced
- 1 red pepper, deseeded and cut into chunks
- 3 spring onions, halved lengthways and cut into long pieces
- 2 handfuls frozen peas
- 2 tbsp chopped coriander leaves
- rice or noodles, to serve

1 In a medium pan, stir the curry paste over the heat for a few seconds, then pour in the coconut milk and bring to the boil.

2 Add the chicken and veg, let everything start to bubble again, then turn down the heat and cook very gently for 5 minutes until the chicken is tender but the vegetables still have some crunch. Stir in the coriander and serve spooned over boiled rice or noodles.

*PER SERVING 544 kcals, protein 40g, carbs 15g, fat 40g, sat fat 30g, fibre 4g, sugar 12g, salt 1.88g*

# Sweet potato & pea curry

Kids love this curry because of the bright colours and the flavour of the sweet potatoes; it's easily doubled if you're feeding a crowd.

 30 minutes    4    Easily doubled

- 3 tbsp curry paste from a jar (use your favourite)
- 1 onion, finely chopped
- 450g/1lb potatoes, cut into chunks
- 2 large sweet potatoes (about 900g/2lb total), cut into chunks
- 600ml/1 pint vegetable stock
- 400ml can coconut milk
- 175g/6oz frozen peas
- few coriander sprigs, roughly chopped, to garnish
- plain boiled rice, to serve

1 Heat the curry paste in a large pan with a lid and stir in the onion. Cover and cook for 5 minutes, stirring occasionally, until softened. Add all the potatoes, the stock and coconut milk to the pan and bring to the boil.

2 Turn the heat down and simmer the curry for 20 minutes until the potato has softened, adding the peas for the final 2 minutes. Season to taste and spoon the curry into bowls, scattering over the coriander before you tuck in. Serve with plain boiled rice.

*PER SERVING 513 kcals, protein 11g, carbs 77g, fat 20g, sat fat 14g, fibre 10g, sugar none, salt 1.46g*

# Smoked haddock & creamed-corn curry

· · · · · · · · · · · · · · · · · · · ·

Everyone will love this creamy fish curry – it is mildly spiced and its heat is cooled with coconut and sweetcorn. It's a great dish on a budget too.

🕐 30 minutes    🍴 4

- 325g can sweetcorn, liquid reserved
- 1 tbsp vegetable oil
- 1 onion, roughly chopped
- 1 tbsp mild curry powder
- 1 garlic clove, crushed
- 50g sachet creamed coconut, chopped
- 4 frozen smoked haddock fillets
- boiled rice, to serve

1 In a blender, whizz the sweetcorn, along with any liquid from the can, into a rough purée and set aside.

2 Heat the oil in a large lidded frying pan and cook the onion for 2–3 minutes to soften. Add the curry powder and garlic, and cook for 1 minute more until fragrant.

3 Tip the creamed coconut into the pan with 300ml/½ pint water, stirring until the creamed coconut dissolves. Add the puréed sweetcorn and bring to the boil. Put the haddock fillets in the sauce, then reduce the heat to a simmer. Cover and cook for 10 minutes, or until the fish is cooked through. Season and serve with boiled rice.

· · · · · · · · · · · · · · · · · · · · · · · ·

*PER SERVING 332 kcals, protein 32g, carbs 23g, fat 13g, sat fat 1g, fibre 3g, sugar 8g, salt 3.4g*

# Indian 'beans on toast'

Quick and colourful, this variation on a classic will fill up the whole family.

🕐 20 minutes    🍽 4

- 2 tbsp vegetable oil
- 2 medium onions, cut into thin wedges
- 1 tsp ground turmeric
- 1 rounded tsp ground cumin
- 4 medium tomatoes, cut into rough chunks
- 410g can green lentils, drained and rinsed
- 4 plain or garlic and coriander, naan breads
- handful coriander leaves, roughly chopped
- few dollops natural yogurt, to garnish
- lemon wedges, to squeeze over

1 Heat the oil in a frying pan. Tip in the onions and cook until really golden, about 5–8 minutes. Stir in the turmeric and cumin for a minute, then add the tomatoes, and cook briefly, moving them around in the pan until they just start to soften but don't lose their shape.

2 Tip in the lentils and heat through for a minute or so. While the lentils are warming, tear the naan breads roughly in half and toast them under the grill or in the toaster – just to warm them through and soften but not brown.

3 Stir 3–4 tablespoons water into the lentils to make a little sauce, warm through, then stir in the coriander and some seasoning. Spoon the lentils over the naan, top with a dollop of yogurt and add a lemon wedge on the side for squeezing over.

*PER SERVING 440 kcals, protein 14g, carbs 64g, fat 16g, sat fat 6g, fibre 5g, sugar 2g, salt 1.05g*

# Thai prawn, squash & pineapple curry

. . . . . . . . . . . . . . . . . . . . .

Have a crowd to feed? Make this colourful curry with coconut milk and Asian aromatics.

🕐 30 minutes  🥘 8

- 200g/8oz Thai curry paste
- 50ml/2fl oz Thai fish sauce
- 600g/1lb 4oz butternut squash, peeled and cubed
- 2 x 400ml cans coconut milk
- 400ml/14fl oz chicken stock
- 400g/14oz pineapple chunks (fresh or from a can)
- 400g/14oz sliced bamboo shoots
- 10 kaffir lime leaves, torn
- 600g/1lb 4oz raw peeled prawns
- bunch Thai basil or coriander, leaves picked
- lime wedges and sliced green chillies, to garnish (optional)

1 In your largest pan or wok, stir the curry paste for a few minutes until fragrant. Add the fish sauce and cook for 1 minute more.

2 Stir in the squash, add the coconut milk and stock, then bring to the boil. Add the pineapple, bamboo shoots and lime leaves. Cook for 15 minutes or until the squash is soft. Add the prawns and Thai basil to the curry and simmer for 1 minute more. Leave to rest for 5 minutes, then taste for seasoning. Serve with lime wedges and green chillies, if you like.

. . . . . . . . . . . . . . . . . . . . . . . .
*PER SERVING 292 kcals, protein 19g, carbs 16g, fat 17g, sat fat 13g, fibre 4g, sugar 10g, salt 2.4g*

# Spicy prawn laksa

A laksa is a curried noodle soup from Malaysia that can be made with vegetables, tofu, chicken, fish, seafood – whatever takes your fancy.

🕐 20 minutes    🍳 4

- 1 tbsp sunflower oil
- 300g bag mixed crunchy stir-fry vegetables
- 140g/5oz shiitake mushrooms, sliced
- 2 tbsp Thai green curry paste
- 400ml can reduced-fat coconut milk
- 200ml/7fl oz vegetable or fish stock
- 300g/10oz medium straight-to-wok noodles
- 200g/8oz large raw peeled prawns

1 Heat a wok, add the oil, then stir-fry the mixed veg and mushrooms for 2–3 minutes. Remove the veg and mushrooms to a plate.
2 Tip the curry paste into the wok and fry for 1 minute. Pour in the coconut milk and stock. Bring to the boil, drop in the noodles and prawns, then reduce the heat and simmer for 4 minutes until the prawns are cooked through. Stir the veg and mushrooms back in, then serve ladled into bowls.

*PER SERVING 327 kcals, protein 16g, carbs 32g, fat 17g, sat fat 10g, fibre 4g, sugar 4g, salt 0.97g*

# Four-spice lamb curry

. . . . . . . . . . . . . . . . . . . . . . .

When you find cumin in a recipe it's often hand-in-hand with coriander; their flavours really complement each other, and particularly so in this four-spice curry.

🕐 30 minutes   🖐 4

- 2 tbsp sunflower oil
- 1 large onion, very finely chopped
- 1 tsp each chilli flakes and ground ginger
- 2 tsp each ground coriander and ground cumin
- 500g/1lb 2oz lean lamb neck fillet, cubed
- 1 large red pepper, deseeded and cubed
- 1 lamb stock cube
- 3 tomatoes, cut into wedges
- 410g can chickpeas, drained and rinsed
- a little chopped coriander, to garnish (optional)

1 Heat the oil in a wok, then fry the onion for about 4 minutes until soft. Stir in the spices, reserving 1 teaspoon of the cumin, then fry for a few seconds more. Toss in the lamb and pepper, and stir-fry over a high heat until the meat has browned.

2 Stir in 200ml/7fl oz water, crumble in the stock cube, season well, then cover and cook for about 6 minutes until the mixture is pulpy and the meat tender. Stir in the tomatoes, chickpeas and remaining spoonful of cumin, and heat through for 2 minutes. If the sauce is too thick, add a splash of water to thin it a little. Serve scattered with the coriander, if using.

. . . . . . . . . . . . . . . . . . . . . . . .
*PER SERVING 439 kcals, protein 31g, carbs 21g, fat 26g, sat fat 10g, fibre 5g, sugar none, salt 0.47g*

# Curried corn & coconut soup

A lovely winter warmer to serve with hot naan bread or chapattis on the side.

🕐 30 minutes    🍴 4–6

- 25g/1oz butter
- 1 onion, chopped
- 1 garlic clove, chopped
- ½ thumb-sized knob ginger, chopped
- 2 tbsp hot Madras curry paste or powder
- 600ml/1 pint chicken stock
- 400ml can coconut milk
- 2 x 300g cans sweetcorn, drained
- 2 tbsp Greek yogurt
- 1 tsp garam masala
- few coriander leaves, to garnish

1 Melt the butter in a pan over a low heat and cook the onion, garlic and ginger until soft. Add the curry paste or powder and stir for 2 minutes. Pour in the stock, coconut milk, half the sweetcorn and some seasoning. Bring to the boil, reduce the heat and simmer for 10 minutes.

2 Pour the soup into a food processor or blender, and blend until smooth. Return to the pan, stir in the remaining sweetcorn and heat through. Ladle into bowls, swirl with yogurt, dust with garam masala and garnish with a little coriander.

*PER SERVING (4) 403 kcals, protein 7g, carbs 39g, fat 25g, sat fat 18g, fibre 2g, sugar 9g, salt 2.04g*

# South Indian egg curry

Try something new with this aromatic, vegetarian, tomato-based curry packed with boiled eggs and served with basmati rice.

🕐 30 minutes   🍴 4

- 4 tbsp vegetable oil
- 1½ tsp mustard seeds
- 1½ tbsp fresh curry leaves
- 2 large red onions, chopped
- 50g/2oz ginger, peeled and finely chopped
- 1 tsp turmeric powder
- ½ tsp chilli powder
- 2 x 400g cans chopped tomatoes
- 1–2 tsp sugar
- 8 eggs
- small bunch coriander, chopped
- rice, mango chutney, natural yogurt and naan bread, to serve (optional)

1 Heat the oil in a wok or medium pan with a lid, then toss in the mustard seeds followed by the curry leaves. Once the leaves have stopped spluttering, reduce the heat and add the onions and ginger. Fry over a medium heat for about 10 minutes until golden.

2 Stir in the turmeric and chilli powder, and cook for a few more seconds. Tip in the tomatoes and sugar. Simmer, uncovered, for 10–15 minutes until thickened, adding a splash of water, if needed. Meanwhile, boil the eggs for 8 minutes, then cool under cold running water before peeling and halving. Add eggs to the curry and cover with a tight-fitting lid.

3 Stir the coriander into the curry. Serve with rice, mango chutney, yogurt and naan bread, if you like.

*PER SERVING 317 kcals, protein 16g, carbs 13g, fat 23g, sat fat 5g, fibre 3g, sugar 10g, salt 0.6g*

# Chicken katsu

Katsu is a Japanese method of breadcrumbing chicken- this version is served with a rich curry sauce

 40 minutes    4

- 4 skinless chicken breasts
- 1 large egg, beaten
- 8 tbsp finely crushed cornflakes or panko crumbs
- 2 garlic cloves, crushed
- 1-2 tbsp Korma paste
- 1 tbsp soy sauce
- 4 tbsp ketchup
- 2 tbsp honey
- 2 tbsp cornflour

1 Heat oven to 200C/180C fan/gas 6. Dip the chicken in the egg, then coat in the cornflakes or crumbs. Space the chicken out on a non-stick baking tray and cook for 15-20 minutes or until cooked through.
2 Put the remaining ingredients in a pan. Pour in 500ml water and heat, stirring, until boiling and thickened. Cover and leave to simmer for 5 minutes.
3 Spoon some sauce onto 4 plates, slice the chicken breasts and place on top. Great served with some rice and soya beans with finely sliced red chilli.

*PER SERVING Kcals 319, protein 34g, carbs 36g, fat 5g, sat fat 1g, fibre none, sugar 13g, salt 2g*

# New potato & mince curry

A light curry that's perfect for spring or summer eating.

🕐 1 hour    🍴 4

- 450g/1lb minced turkey
- 1 tbsp vegetable oil
- 1 small onion, chopped
- 3 garlic cloves, finely chopped
- 1 tbsp coarsely grated ginger
- 1 red chilli, deseeded and finely sliced
- 2 tsp each ground cumin and coriander
- 1 tbsp korma curry paste
- 500g/1lb 2oz new potatoes, halved
- 100g/4oz spinach leaves
- 150g/5oz Greek yogurt
- chapattis or naan bread, to serve

1 Heat a frying pan and dry-fry the mince. Brown it all over, stirring to break it up. Remove from the pan to a plate. Add the oil and onion to the pan, and cook for 5 minutes.

2 Stir in the garlic, ginger, chilli, spices and curry paste. Stir-fry for 1 minute. Add the mince, potatoes and 600ml/1 pint water, bring to the boil, cover, then simmer for 30 minutes. Season with salt to taste.

3 Stir in the spinach and simmer for 1 minute, uncovered, until wilted. Swirl through the yogurt and serve with Indian bread.

*PER SERVING 315 kcals, protein 32g, carbs 25g, fat 10g, sat fat 3g, fibre 2g, sugar 4g, salt 0.55g*

# Easy-peasy lentil curry

· · · · · · · · · · · · · · · · · · · · ·

Packed full of lentils, vegetables and dried fruit, you won't be left feeling hungry after this low-fat curry.

🕐 35–40 minutes   🥧 4

- 2 tbsp sunflower oil
- 2 medium onions, cut into rough wedges
- 4 tbsp curry paste
- 850ml/1½ pints vegetable stock
- 750g/1lb 10oz mixed veg (such as carrots, parsnips and sweet potatoes), peeled and cut into small chunks
- 100g/4oz red split lentils
- 200g/8oz basmati rice
- ¼ tsp turmeric powder
- handful raisins
- handful roughly chopped parsley leaves
- poppadums and mango chutney, to serve

1 Heat the oil in a large pan. Add the onions and cook over a high heat for about 8 minutes or until golden brown. Stir in the curry paste for a minute then pour in a little of the stock so it sizzles, scraping any bits from the bottom of the pan. Pour in the rest of the stock.

2 Stir in the vegetables, cover and simmer for 5 minutes. Add the lentils and simmer for a further 15–20 minutes or until cooked.

3 While the curry is simmering, cook the rice according to the pack instructions, adding the turmeric to the cooking water. Drain well.

4 Season the curry, toss in the raisins and the chopped parsley, then serve with the rice, and some poppadums and mango chutney.

· · · · · · · · · · · · · · · · · · · · · ·

*PER SERVING 432 kcals, protein 14g, carbs 76g, fat 10g, sat fat 1g, fibre 6g, sugar none, salt 1.38g*

# Tamarind chickpeas

This superhealthy recipe is great for vegetarians as it is packed full of spinach, which is a good source of iron.

🕐 25–35 minutes   🍴 2

- 1 tbsp vegetable or sunflower oil
- ½ tsp kalonji seeds (also known as black onion or nigella seeds)
- 1 tsp fennel seeds
- 1 medium onion, chopped
- 400g can chopped tomatoes
- 3 green chillies, deseeded and cut into quarters lengthways
- 2–3 tsp light muscovado sugar
- 1 tsp each paprika and ground turmeric
- 410g can chickpeas, drained and rinsed
- 1 tbsp tamarind paste
- 1 tbsp chopped coriander leavesr
- ½ x 250g bag baby leaf spinach
- natural yogurt and chapattis, to serve

1. Heat the oil in a pan, fry the kalonji and fennel seeds for about 10 seconds. Add the onion and cook gently for 8–10 minutes until lightly golden.
2. Mix in the tomatoes, chillies, sugar, paprika, turmeric and chickpeas. Bring to the boil, then simmer for 10 minutes. Stir in the tamarind and coriander. Add the spinach leaves and stir gently until they've just wilted. Serve with yogurt and chapattis.

*PER SERVING 334 kcals, protein 16g, carbs 45g, fat 11g, sat fat 1g, fibre 9g, sugar 5g, salt 1.34g*

# Fragrant chicken curry with chickpeas

By whizzing the ingredients to a paste first, they can cook without needing oil.

🕐 1 hour    🍽 4

- 2 onions, quartered
- 3 fat garlic cloves
- ½ x finger-length knob ginger, roughly chopped
- 2 tbsp medium curry powder
- ½ tsp turmeric powder
- 2 tsp paprika
- 1 red chilli, seeded and roughly chopped
- 1 small bunch coriander
- 425ml/¾ pint chicken stock
- 4 boneless skinless chicken breasts, cubed
- 410g can chickpeas, drained and rinsed
- low-fat natural yogurt, rice and poppadums, to serve

1 Tip the onions, garlic, ginger, curry powder, turmeric, paprika, chilli and half of the coriander into a food processor. Add 1 teaspoon salt and blend to a purée. Tip the mixture into a pan and cook over a low heat for 10 minutes, stirring frequently.

2 Pour in the stock and bring to the boil. Add the chicken, then lower the heat and simmer for 20 minutes until tender.

3 Chop the remaining coriander and stir most of it into the curry with the chickpeas. Heat through. Sprinkle with the reserved coriander, and serve with yogurt, rice and poppadums.

*PER SERVING 272 kcals, protein 39g, carbs 19g, fat 5g, sat fat 1g, fibre 5g, sugar none, salt 1.68g*

# Spiced rice & lentils with cauliflower

Lentils contain useful amounts of zinc, iron and calcium as well as cholesterol-lowering fibre; combine them with peas and you will increase the iron you absorb.

🕐 45 minutes  🥧 4

- 2 tbsp sunflower oil
- 1 onion, chopped
- 2 carrots, chopped
- 200g/8oz basmati rice
- 50g/2oz red split lentils
- 3 rounded tbsp korma curry paste
- 1 cauliflower, cut into florets
- 100g/4oz frozen peas
- a few toasted cashew nuts, to garnish
- natural yogurt and mango chutney, to serve

1 Heat the oil in a pan, add the onion and carrots, then fry for 5 minutes until lightly coloured. Stir in the rice and lentils, cook for 1 more minute, add the curry paste and 900ml/1½ pints water, then bring to the boil. Cover, then simmer for 10 minutes.

2 Stir in the cauliflower, then cook for 10 minutes more until the rice and lentils are tender. Add the peas 2 minutes before the cooking time is up, stirring them through. Top with the nuts, then serve in bowls with yogurt and mango chutney.

# Superquick fish curry

This low-fat curry can be on the table in only 15 minutes from scratch.

🕐 15 minutes    🍳 4

- 1 tbsp vegetable oil
- 1 large onion, chopped
- 1 garlic clove, chopped
- 1–2 tbsp Madras curry paste
- 400g can chopped tomatoes
- 200ml/7fl oz vegetable stock
- 600g/1lb 5oz white fish fillet, skinned and cut into big chunks
- rice or naan bread, to serve

1 Heat the oil in a deep pan and gently fry the onion and garlic for about 5 minutes until soft. Add the curry paste and stir-fry for 1–2 minutes, then tip in the tomatoes and stock.

2 Bring to a simmer, then add the fish. Gently cook for 4–5 minutes until the fish flakes easily. Serve immediately with rice or naan bread.

*PER SERVING 191 kcals, protein 30g, carbs 8g, fat 5g, sat fat 1g, fibre 2g, sugar 6g, salt 0.54g*

# Fruity chicken & coconut curry

Not only is this curry healthy, it also uses up leftover cooked chicken – perfect for a Monday-night dinner.

🕐 35 minutes   🍴 4

- 200g/8oz long grain, Thai or basmati rice
- 1 tbsp sunflower oil
- 2 courgettes, cut into chunks
- 1 red pepper, deseeded and cut into chunks
- 375g/13oz skinless cooked chicken, chopped into chunks
- 1 bunch spring onions, finely sliced
- 100ml/3½fl oz reduced-fat coconut milk
- 150ml/¼ pint chicken stock
- 1 tbsp Thai red curry paste
- 1 orange, segmented

1 Cook the rice in boiling water according to the pack instructions.
2 Meanwhile, heat the oil in a wok or large frying pan and add the courgettes and pepper. Stir-fry over a high heat for 3 minutes until just starting to brown. Add the chicken and cook, stirring, for 2 minutes.
3 Toss in the spring onions and pour over the coconut milk, stock and curry paste. Heat until simmering then cook, uncovered, for 5–6 minutes.
4 Add the orange segments to the chicken mixture. Heat for 1–2 minutes, then season. Drain the rice and divide the rice and the curry among four warmed plates.

*PER SERVING 445 kcals, protein 30g, carbs 58g, fat 11g, sat fat 4g, fibre 2g, sugar none, salt 0.8g*

# Spicy pork & aubergine curry

You don't have to avoid pork if you're trying to eat healthily, just choose a leaner cut, such as the fillet.

🕐 40 minutes   🍽 4

- 4 tsp olive oil
- 2 onions, sliced
- 1 aubergine, diced
- 500g/1lb 2oz lean pork fillet, trimmed of any fat and sliced
- 2 red peppers, deseeded and cut into chunky strips
- 2–3 tbsp mild curry powder
- 400g can plum tomatoes
- basmati rice, to serve

1 Heat the oil in a large non-stick frying pan with a lid. Tip in the onions and aubergine, and fry for 8 minutes, stirring frequently, until soft and golden brown.

2 Tip in the pork and fry for 5 minutes, stirring occasionally, until starting to brown. Mix in the pepper strips and stir-fry for about 3 minutes until soft.

3 Sprinkle in the curry powder. Stir-fry for a minute, then pour in the tomatoes and 150ml/¼ pint water. Stir vigorously, cover the pan and leave the mixture to simmer for 5 minutes until the tomatoes break down to form a thick sauce – you can add a drop more water, if the mixture gets too thick. Season with some salt and pepper, and serve with basmati rice.

# Low-fat prawn & almond korma

This curry has all the flavour of a korma without the rich, creamy sauce.

🕐 20 minutes    🍽 4

- 1 tbsp sunflower oil
- 1 onion, chopped
- 400g pack frozen raw peeled prawns, defrosted
- 2 tbsp korma curry paste
- 3 tbsp ground almonds
- handful coriander leaves, roughly chopped, to garnish
- rice, to serve

1 Heat the oil in a frying pan, add the onion, then fry for 5 minutes until lightly coloured.
2 Add the prawns, then stir quickly until they are evenly pink. Stir in the curry paste, then add 150ml/¼ pint water and the ground almonds. Bring to the boil, then simmer for 2–3 minutes until the sauce is slightly thickened. Scatter with the chopped coriander and serve with rice.

# Squash, spinach & black-bean dopiaza

Just one portion of this curry provides all five of your 5-a-day target.

⏱ 40 minutes   🍽 2

- 2 onions, thinly sliced
- 2 tbsp sunflower oil
- 1 garlic clove, crushed
- 1 tsp each ground cumin, ground coriander and curry powder
- pinch chilli powder
- 400g/14oz butternut squash (peeled weight), cut into chunks
- 1 tbsp tomato purée
- 410g can black beans in water, drained and rinsed
- 200g/8oz spinach leaves, washed

1 Heat oven to 190C/170C fan/gas 5. Toss half the onions in 1 tablespoon of the oil, then tip into a roasting tin and roast in the oven for 15–20 minutes until crisp and golden. Set aside.

2 Meanwhile, fry the remaining onion in a lidded pan in the rest of the oil until lightly golden. Add the garlic and spices, and cook for 1 minute. Add the squash, stir in the tomato purée and 425ml/¾ pint boiling water, then return to the boil. Simmer, covered, for 15 minutes, then stir in the beans. Cook for a further 5 minutes.

3 Put the spinach in a colander and pour over a kettle of boiling water until wilted. Press with a wooden spoon to remove excess water, then roughly chop. Stir into the curry, then warm through. Serve scattered with the crisp roasted onions.

*PER SERVING 354 kcals, protein 17g, carbs 42g, fat 14g, sat fat 2g, fibre 13g, sugar 14g, salt 0.51g*

# Low-fat chicken curry

You can grate and chop your own ginger and chillies, if you like, but this is a curry for someone in a hurry.

🕐 15 minutes    🍽 2

- 1 tbsp sunflower oil
- 1 red onion, thinly sliced
- 1 garlic clove, crushed
- 2 tsp minced ginger, from a jar
- ½–1 tsp chopped red chillies, from a jar
- ½ x 400g can chopped tomatoes
- 200g/8oz boneless skinless chicken breasts, chopped into chunks
- 2 tsp garam masala
- 3 tbsp low-fat natural yogurt, plus extra to garnish (optional)
- handful coriander leaves, roughly chopped, to garnish
- garlic and coriander naans, plus cucumber, lettuce and red onion salad, to serve

1 Heat the oil in a pan, add the onion and fry until softened. Add the garlic, ginger and chilli, and cook briefly. Add the tomatoes and a quarter of the can of water, and bring to the boil. Simmer for 2 minutes, then add the chicken and garam masala, cover and cook for another 6–8 minutes until the chicken is cooked through.

2 Reduce the heat to a simmer, then stir in the yogurt. Sprinkle with coriander and serve with an extra spoon of yogurt, if you like, alongside warm garlic and coriander naans and a crisp salad of cucumber, shredded lettuce and sliced red onion.

*PER SERVING 248 kcals, protein 29g, carbs 16g, fat 8g, sat fat 1g, fibre 3g, sugar 11g, salt 0.5g*

# Lentil & sweet-potato curry

A storecupboard spice pot with red and green lentils, chickpeas and coriander. Serve with seasoned yogurt and naan bread.

🕐 35 minutes    🥧 2

- 2 tbsp vegetable or olive oil
- 1 red onion, chopped
- 1 tsp cumin seeds
- 1 tsp mustard seeds (any colour)
- 1 tbsp medium curry powder
- 100g/4oz red split or green lentils, or a mixture
- 2 medium sweet potatoes, peeled and cut into chunks
- 500ml/17fl oz vegetable stock
- 400g can chopped tomatoes
- 400g can chickpeas, drained and rinsed
- ¼ small pack coriander (optional)
- seasoned yogurt and naan breads, to serve

1 Heat the oil in a large pan, add the onion and cook for a few minutes until softened. Add the seeds and curry powder, and cook for 1 minute more, then stir in the lentils, sweet potatoes, stock and chopped tomatoes.

2 Bring to the boil, then cover and simmer for 20 minutes until the lentils and sweet potatoes are tender. Add the chickpeas, then heat through. Season and serve sprinkled with coriander, if you like, and some seasoned yogurt and naan bread alongside.

*PER SERVING 613 kcals, protein 27g, carbs 91g, fat 18g, sat fat 2g, fibre 16g, sugar 21g, salt 1.8g*

# Warming veggie curry

A good source of vitamin C, this low-fat curry also counts for two of your 5-a-day target.

🕐 35 minutes   🍴 4

- 1 tbsp sunflower oil
- 1 butternut squash, peeled and cut into chunks
- 1 onion, sliced
- 1 tbsp Thai red curry paste
- 50g sachet creamed coconut
- 250g/9oz frozen French beans
- warmed naan bread, to serve

1 Heat the oil in a pan. Tip in the squash and onion, then gently fry for about 5 minutes until the onion is soft, but not browned. Tip in the curry paste and cook for 1 minute more.
2 Mix the creamed coconut together with 300ml/½ pint boiling water, then pour into the pan. Bring to the boil and simmer for 10 minutes.
3 Add the beans to the pan, then cook for about 3–5 minutes more until everything is just tender. Serve with warmed naan bread.

*PER SERVING 178 kcals, protein 5g, carbs 23g, fat 9g, sat fat 4g, fibre 5g, sugar 13g, salt 0.17g*

# Light chicken korma

A mild curry that gets its creaminess from a last-minute swirl of fromage frais.

 35 minutes  🥘 4

- small knob ginger, finely sliced
- 1 garlic clove, crushed
- 1 onion, sliced
- 1 tbsp vegetable oil
- 4 boneless skinless chicken breasts, cut into bite-sized pieces
- 1 tsp garam masala
- 100ml/3½fl oz chicken stock
- 3 tbsp low-fat fromage frais
- 2 tbsp ground almonds
- handful toasted and sliced almonds and some chopped coriander leaves, to garnish
- rice and chapattis or naan bread, to serve

1 Cook the ginger, garlic and onion in a large pan with the oil until softened. Tip in the chicken and cook until lightly browned, about 5 minutes, then add the garam masala and cook for 1 minute more. Pour over the stock and simmer for 10 minutes until the chicken is cooked through.

2 Mix together the fromage frais and ground almonds in a small bowl. Take the pan off the heat and stir in the fromage-frais mixture. Sprinkle over the sliced almonds, garnish with coriander and serve with rice and chapattis or plain naan bread, if you like.

*PER SERVING 243 kcals, protein 37g, carbs 4g, fat 9g, sat fat 1g, fibre 1g, sugar 3g, salt 0.31g*

# Spiced chickpea & potato fry-up

Scoop this low-fat but hearty curry into bowls and eat with a spoon.

 30 minutes    4

- 300g/10oz potatoes, cut into small pieces
- 2 onions, sliced
- 2 garlic cloves, crushed
- 1 tsp olive oil
- 1 tsp each ground coriander, and turmeric and mild chilli powder
- 1 tbsp cumin seeds
- 410g can chickpeas, drained and rinsed
- 2 tbsp tomato purée
- 200g/8oz baby leaf spinach
- 1 small bunch coriander, leaves chopped
- wholemeal chapattis, low-fat natural yogurt and mango chutney, to serve

1 Boil the potatoes in a pan of salted water until just tender. While they are cooking, soften the onions and garlic in the oil in a frying pan for a few minutes. Add all the spices, then fry for 1 minute more. Stir in the chickpeas and tomato purée along with 400ml/14fl oz water, then turn up the heat and bubble for a few minutes.

2 When the potatoes are ready, drain them and add to the frying pan. Cook for a few minutes until the sauce is thick, stir in the spinach, then season.

3 When the spinach has wilted, stir in the coriander and serve with the chapattis, yogurt and chutney on the side.

*PER SERVING 201 kcals, protein 10g, carbs 33g, fat 4g, sat fat none, fibre 6g, sugar 6g, salt 0.66g*

# Slow-cooked beetroot & beef curry

This Pakistani curry has a deep purple hue and is flavoured with fragrant cinnamon, cumin and coriander.

🕐 1 hour 50 minutes     🍴 3

- 3–4 tbsp corn or sunflower oil
- 1 black cardamom pod (preferable) or 3 green
- 2.5cm/1in cinnamon stick
- 1 tsp cumin seeds
- 1 tsp coriander seeds
- 2 medium red onions, sliced
- 1 tsp grated garlic
- 1 tsp grated ginger
- 2 medium tomatoes, chopped
- 1 tsp red chilli powder
- 450g/1lb lean stewing beef, cut into 2.5cm/1in chunks
- 350g/12oz raw beetroot, grated
- small pack coriander, leaves picked
- 1 green chilli, chopped
- squeeze ½ lime
- naan bread or basmati rice, to serve

1  Using a large non-stick lidded wok or pan, heat the oil over a medium heat, add the cardamom, cinnamon, cumin and coriander seeds. Once the spices start to sizzle, add the onions and stir-fry until light golden brown. Add the garlic and ginger, and cook for 1 minute until it no longer smells raw. Add a splash of water, if the garlic and ginger start to stick to the pan, then add the tomatoes and cook until soft.

2  Add 1 teaspoon salt, the chilli powder and beef, turn up the heat and stir-fry until the meat is sealed on all sides. Cover loosely and cook for 10 minutes on a medium-low heat.

3  Turn up the heat and add the beetroot. Stir-fry for a few minutes, then cover the pan, reduce the heat and cook for 1¼ hours or until the meat is tender. Stir from time to time and add a little water, if it becomes dry.

4  Once the beef is tender and the beetroot softened, sprinkle with the coriander leaves and green chilli; add a squeeze of lime, and serve with naan or basmati rice.

*PER SERVING 472 kcals, protein 36g, carbs 17g, fat 28g, sat fat 7g, fibre 5g, sugar 14g, salt 2.1g*

# Red pork curry with green beans

Thai red curry paste is a concentrated mixture of herbs and spices, flavoured with dried red chillies.

🕐 30–40 minutes   🍽 4

- 250g/9oz green beans, trimmed and halved
- 1 tbsp vegetable oil
- 4 tsp Thai red curry paste
- 1 tbsp finely chopped ginger
- 500g/1lb 2oz pork fillet, thinly sliced
- 300ml/½ pint vegetable stock
- 2 tbsp Thai fish sauce
- 1 tsp light muscovado sugar
- 400ml can coconut milk
- 400g can palm hearts, drained, rinsed and sliced
- grated zest and juice 1 large lime
- handful each basil and coriander leaves
- rice noodles, to serve

1 Cook the beans in boiling salted water for 5 minutes, then drain and refresh under cold running water. Set aside.
2 Heat the oil in a pan, add the curry paste and ginger, and fry gently until the oil separates out. Tip in the pork and stock, bring to the boil, then simmer for 5 minutes.
3 Add the fish sauce, sugar, coconut milk, palm hearts, lime zest and juice, and simmer for a further 5 minutes, adding the beans halfway through. Throw in the basil and coriander, and serve with rice noodles.

*PER SERVING 396 kcals, protein 32g, carbs 10g, fat 26g, sat fat 16g, fibre 2g, sugar 1g, salt 2.29g*

# Prawn & coconut curry

Creamy and mild, gently spiced coconut curries are always a popular choice on any menu.

🕐 30 minutes  🥧 2

- 4 tsp vegetable oil
- 1 tsp mustard seeds
- 1 small onion, finely chopped
- 1 tbsp finely chopped ginger
- 1 garlic clove, finely chopped
- ¼ tsp each turmeric and mild chilli powder
- ½ tsp ground coriander
- 2 fresh bay leaves
- 1 small green chilli, deseeded and thinly sliced
- 10 raw peeled king prawns
- 200ml carton coconut cream
- 1 lime, halved

1 Heat the oil in a frying pan. Fry the mustard seeds until they pop. Tip in the onion and fry, stirring, until golden. Add the ginger and garlic, and cook for 1 minute, then add the turmeric, chilli powder and coriander, and cook for 30 seconds more. Add the bay leaves and chilli, and cook for 1 minute.

2 Pour in 150ml/¼ pint water and bubble for a minute. Stir in the prawns. Lower the heat and simmer for 3–4 minutes, until the prawns are cooked.

3 Pour in the coconut cream, warm through, then squeeze in the juice from one of the lime halves. Season with salt and serve with the other lime half, cut into wedges.

*PER SERVING 519 kcals, protein 23g, carbs 12g, fat 42g, sat fat 31g, fibre 1g, sugar none, salt 3.08g*

# Beef, potato & banana curry

Banana and tamarind add a rich sweetness to this slow-cooked spice pot in a coconut sauce. Serve with nutty basmati rice.

🕐 3 hours   🍴 4

- 2 tbsp sunflower oil
- 800g/1lb 12oz stewing beef, cut into chunks
- 2 onions, chopped
- 2 lemongrass stalks, bashed
- 2 tbsp grated ginger
- 2 tbsp tamarind paste
- 3 garlic cloves, crushed
- 1 tsp turmeric powder
- 2 tbsp medium curry powder
- 2 tsp brown sugar
- 400ml can coconut milk
- 500g bag new potatoes, halved
- 3 small or 2 large slightly underripe bananas, cut into 2cm/¾in-thick slices
- 2 tsp garam masala
- small pack coriander, leaves picked
- squeeze lemon juice (optional)

1 Heat oven to 180C/160C fan/gas 4 and heat half the oil in a large frying pan. Brown the beef in batches and transfer to a flameproof casserole dish. Add the remaining oil to the pan with the onions and fry gently until softened. Stir in the lemongrass, ginger, tamarind, garlic, turmeric, curry powder and sugar, and fry for a few minutes until fragrant. Add the coconut milk with a can of water, stir into the beef and bring to a simmer. Cover and bake for 1 hour.

2 Stir in the new potatoes and cook for 1 hour more until the potatoes are tender, removing the lid halfway through cooking. The casserole can now be cooled and chilled, or frozen for up to 2 months, if preparing ahead.

3 Put the casserole back on the hob. Stir in the bananas and garam masala, and simmer, uncovered, for 10 minutes until the sauce has thickened. Scatter the curry with the coriander, season well, then taste – it may need a squeeze of lemon to finish it off.

*PER SERVING 713 kcals, protein 41g, carbs 53g, fat 36g, sat fat 20g, fibre 5g, sugar 28g, salt 0.2g*

# Vegetable vindaloo

If you like your curries fiery, this is the one for you.

🕐 35 minutes    🍽 4-6

- 1 tbsp sunflower oil
- 3 tbsp vindaloo curry paste
- 1 tbsp soft brown sugar
- juice ½ lemon
- 2 courgettes, thickly sliced
- 300g/10oz cauliflower florets (about ½ a head)
- 400ml/14fl oz passata
- 410g can chickpeas, drained and rinsed
- 250g bag leaf spinach, washed
- basmati rice, to serve

1 Heat the oil in a large pan, add the curry paste and fry for 1 minute. Add the sugar and lemon juice, cook for 1 minute, then tip in the courgettes and cauliflower, and cook for 2 minutes. Now stir in the passata, plus 100ml/3½fl oz water and the chickpeas, then season to taste. Bring to the boil, cover with a lid and simmer for 15 minutes.

2 Just before serving, throw in the spinach, give it a stir and remove the vindaloo from the heat once the leaves have just wilted. Serve with basmati rice.

*PER SERVING (4) 142 kcals, protein 8g, carbs 16g, fat 6g, sat fat none, fibre 4g, sugar 8g, salt 1.01g*

# Thai green chicken curry

This is the ultimate Thai classic; this recipe can be easily reproduced at home and is just as delicious as a good restaurant version.

🕐 30–35 minutes    🍽 6

- 200g/8oz new potatoes, cut into chunks
- 100g/4oz green beans, trimmed and halved
- 1 tbsp sunflower oil
- 1 garlic clove, chopped
- 1 rounded tbsp Thai green curry paste
- 400ml can coconut milk
- 2 tsp Thai fish sauce
- 1 tsp caster sugar
- 450g/1lb skinless chicken breasts, cut into pieces
- 3 fresh kaffir lime leaves, finely shredded, or dried ones, crushed
- good handful basil leaves
- rice, to serve

1 Boil the potatoes for 5 minutes, then throw in the beans and cook for a further 3 minutes, by which time both should be just tender. Drain the veg and set aside.

2 In a wok or large frying pan, heat the oil until very hot, then drop in the garlic and cook for a few seconds until golden. Add the curry paste for a few more seconds just to begin to cook the spices. Next, pour in the coconut milk and let it come to a bubble.

3 Stir in the fish sauce, sugar and chicken pieces. Simmer, covered, for about 8 minutes until the chicken is cooked.

4 Tip in the potatoes and beans, and warm through, then stir in most of the shredded or crushed lime leaves and the basil, and remove from the heat. Scatter with the remaining lime leaves and serve with rice.

*PER SERVING 245 kcals, protein 20g, carbs 10g, fat 14g, sat fat 10g, fibre 1g, sugar 4g, salt 0.82g*

# Spiced broccoli with paneer

Paneer cheese makes a great ingredient for vegetarian curries. This one is spiced up with garam masala.

🕐 20 minutes   🥧 2

- 1 large head broccoli, broken into florets
- 1 tbsp olive oil
- 225g pack paneer, sliced
- 1 tsp garam masala
- 1 garlic clove, finely chopped
- 1 red chilli, deseeded and finely chopped
- zest and juice 1 lemon
- warm naan bread, to serve

1 Cook the broccoli in a large pan of boiling salted water for 3–4 minutes. Save a little of the cooking water, then drain the broccoli into a colander.

2 Heat the oil in a large frying pan over a medium heat. Season, then fry the paneer for 2–3 minutes on each side until golden. Move the paneer to the edge of the pan and add the garam masala, garlic, chilli and reserved cooking water. Cook for 2 minutes, then return the broccoli to the pan, with the lemon zest and juice. Toss everything together to heat through and serve with warm naan breads.

*PER SERVING 529 kcals, protein 37g, carbs 7g, fat 40g, sat fat 21g, fibre 8g, sugar 4g, salt 1.3g*

# Chicken korma

· · · · · · · · · · · · · · · · · · · · · ·

A real favourite from the take-away menu – and a great mild choice for kids.

🕐 40 minutes    🍽 4

- 2 medium onions
- 4 tbsp sunflower oil
- 4 garlic cloves, crushed or finely chopped
- 1½ tsp garam masala
- ¼–½ tsp cayenne pepper
- 4 skinless chicken breast fillets, cut into chunks
- 500g pot natural yogurt
- 50g/2oz ground almonds
- handful chopped coriander leaves
- basmati rice, to serve

1 Finely chop one of the onions. Heat half the oil in a pan, add the chopped onion and garlic, and cook over a medium heat for 2–3 minutes. Add another tablespoon of oil, stir in the garam masala and cayenne, and continue to cook, stirring, for 1 minute.

2 Add the chicken and cook for a further 2–3 minutes. Stir in the yogurt and ground almonds, and simmer gently for 8–10 minutes or until the chicken is cooked.

3 Meanwhile, thinly slice the remaining onion and heat the remaining tablespoon of oil in a non-stick pan. Fry the onion until browned and crisp. Remove with a slotted spoon and drain on kitchen paper.

4 Stir the coriander and some seasoning into the curry and serve with some basmati rice, scattered with the crispy onions.

· · · · · · · · · · · · · · · · · · · · · · ·
*PER SERVING 458 kcals, protein 45g, carbs 17g, fat 24g, sat fat 5g, fibre 2g, sugar 14g, salt 0.48g*

# Vegetable balti

This is a delicious dish in its own right, but if there are any leftovers it makes a great topping for a jacket potato the next day.

🕐 1½ hours   🍽 4

- 1 tbsp vegetable oil
- 1 large onion, thickly sliced
- 1 large garlic clove, crushed
- 1 eating apple, peeled, cored and chopped into chunks
- 3 tbsp balti curry paste
- 1 medium butternut squash, peeled and cut into chunks
- 2 large carrots, thickly sliced
- 200g/8oz turnips, cut into chunks
- 1 medium cauliflower, broken into florets
- 400g can chopped tomatoes
- 425ml/¾ pint hot vegetable stock
- 4 tbsp chopped coriander leaves, plus extra to sprinkle
- 150g pot natural yogurt
- naan bread, to serve

1 Heat the oil in a very large pan, then add the onion, garlic and apple, and cook gently until softened. Stir in the curry paste.

2 Tip in all the vegetables, the chopped tomatoes and the stock with 3 tablespoons of the coriander. Bring to the boil, then lower the heat, cover and cook for 30 minutes. Uncover and cook for another 20 minutes until the vegetables are soft and the sauce thickened. Season well.

3 Mix 1 tablespoon of the coriander into the yogurt. Ladle the curry into warmed bowls and ripple some yogurt over the top. Sprinkle with extra chopped coriander, then serve with naan on the side.

*PER SERVING 201 kcals, protein 11g, carbs 25g, fat 7g, sat fat 1g, fibre 7g, sugar none, salt 1.13g*

# Vegan vegetable biryani

A meat and dairy-free Indian-inspired basmati-rice dish with cauliflower, French beans, peas, potatoes and a homemade curry paste.

 1 hour 10 minutes    8

- 400g/14oz basmati rice
- 2 tbsp vegetable oil
- 1 cauliflower, cut into florets
- 2 potatoes, cut into chunks
- 100g/4oz red split lentils
- 100g/4oz French beans, trimmed and cut in half
- handful fresh curry leaves
- 2 handfuls frozen peas
- small bunch coriander
- 50g/2oz roasted cashew nuts, roughly chopped
- poppadoms or naan bread and carrot salad, to serve

**FOR THE PASTE**

- 1 large onion, roughly chopped
- large knob ginger, peeled and roughly chopped
- 5 garlic cloves
- 2 tsp curry powder
- 1 tsp ground cumin
- 2 tbsp vegetable oil
- 1 small green chilli

1 Soak the rice in a pan for 30 minutes; rinse in several changes of water until it runs clear. Cover with 1cm/½in water, cover the pan, bring to the boil, stir once, then turn off the heat. Leave for 10 minutes, covered; stir again and leave to stand, covered. Meanwhile, make the paste by blitzing all the ingredients together in a food processor.

2 Heat the oil in a pan. Tip in the paste, then add the cauliflower and potatoes. Cook in the paste then add the lentils and green beans, and cover with 400ml/14fl oz water. Add the curry leaves, season with salt, cover with a lid and simmer for 20 minutes until the lentils and vegetables are tender. Add the peas for the last 2 minutes to defrost. Stir the rice through the curry until completely mixed and hot, then spoon on to a platter and scatter with coriander and cashews.

3 Serve the biryani on a large platter, with carrot salad and poppadoms for any vegans and naan bread for everyone else.

*PER SERVING 424 kcals, protein 14g, carbs 60g, fat 13g, sat fat 2g, fibre 7g, sugar 9g, salt 0.2g*

# Keema curry pies

. . . . . . . . . . . . . . . . . . . .

This is a classic keema curry with a twist – there's no need for rice on the side, as we've turned this dish upside down and topped it with some spicy mash.

🕐 1½ hours    🍴 6

- 1 large onion, chopped
- 2 tbsp sunflower oil
- 2 garlic cloves, crushed
- small knob ginger, grated
- 2 tbsp medium curry powder
- 500g/1lb 2oz minced beef or lamb
- 400g can chopped tomatoes
- 100g/4oz frozen peas

**FOR THE TOPPING**

- 1kg/2lb 4oz mixed parsnips and potatoes, peeled and cut into chunks
- 1 green chilli, deseeded and chopped
- 1 large bunch coriander leaves, chopped
- 2 tsp turmeric powder
- juice 1 lemon
- 50g/2oz butter

1 First, make the keema curry. Cook the onion in the oil until soft. Add the garlic, ginger and curry powder, and cook for 3 minutes, then increase the heat and add the mince. Fry until lightly browned, then add the tomatoes and simmer for about 20 minutes until thickened, throwing in the peas for the final minute.

2 Meanwhile, boil the parsnips and potatoes for the topping until tender. Drain, season and mash with the rest of the topping ingredients.

3 Heat oven to 220C/200C fan/gas 7. Divide the keema curry among six small dishes, or spoon into one large one, and top with mash. Bake for 20 minutes until golden and bubbling.

. . . . . . . . . . . . . . . . . . . . . .

*PER PIE 424 kcals, protein 22g, carbs 27g, fat 26g, sat fat 11g, fibre 8g, sugar 10g, salt 0.53g*

# Speedy green chicken curry

The definition of curry in a hurry, try this fragrant Thai spice-pot with chicken, green beans and basil.

🕐 15 minutes　　◔ 4

- 1 tsp vegetable oil
- 1 red onion, cut into half-moon slices
- 4 tbsp Thai green curry paste
- 2 x 400g cans light coconut milk
- 2 tbsp Thai fish sauce
- zest and juice 2 limes
- 1 tbsp brined green peppercorns, drained and rinsed
- 200g/8oz green beans, trimmed and halved
- 4 skinless chicken breasts, cut into long strips
- handful basil leaves
- basmati rice, to serve

1 Heat the oil in a medium pan, add the onion and fry for 2 minutes. Tip in the paste and cook for 1 minute more. Pour in the coconut milk, fish sauce, lime zest and juice and peppercorns. Bring to a simmer, then add the beans and chicken. Cook for 5 minutes or until the chicken is cooked through.

2 Just before serving, add the basil leaves. Serve with basmati rice.

PER SERVING 352 kcals, protein 35g, carbs 9g, fat 20g, sat fat 13g, fibre 3g, sugar 5g, salt 2.5g

# Spiced vegetable biryani

A biryani is a great all-in-one meal; just serve with raita, if you like.

🕐 1 hour   🍴 6

- 2 tbsp vegetable oil
- 1 small cauliflower, broken into small florets
- 2 large sweet potatoes, peeled and cubed
- 1 large onion, sliced
- 1 litre/1¾ pints hot vegetable stock
- 3 tbsp hot curry paste (Madras is good)
- 1 red chilli, deseeded and finely chopped
- ½ tsp turmeric powder
- 2 tsp mustard seeds (black or white)
- 500g/1lb 2oz basmati rice
- 140g/5oz trimmed green beans, halved
- juice 2 lemons
- handful coriander leaves
- 50g/2oz roasted salted cashew nuts

1 Heat oven to 220C/200C fan/gas 7. Pour the oil into a large ovenproof dish and heat in the oven for 5 minutes. Add all the vegetables, except the beans, stirring to coat in the hot oil. Season and return to the oven for 15 minutes until beginning to brown.

2 Meanwhile, in a bowl, stir together the stock, curry paste, chilli, turmeric and mustard seeds. Mix the rice and green beans into the dish, then pour over the stock mixture. Lower the oven to 190C/170C fan/gas 5. Cover the dish with foil and bake for 30 minutes until the rice is tender and liquid absorbed. Stir in the lemon juice, then scatter over the coriander and cashews, and serve.

*PER SERVING 494 kcals, protein 14g, carbs 89g, fat 12g, sat fat 1g, fibre 5g, sugar none, salt 0.99g*

# Chicken balti one-pot

This chicken balti becomes a one-pan meal with the addition of some quinoa – if you don't fancy using quinoa, just swap it for basmati rice instead.

🕐 35 minutes    🍴 4

- 1 tbsp sunflower oil
- 2 large onions, thickly sliced
- 4 boneless skinless chicken breasts
- 5 tbsp balti paste
- 200g/8oz quinoa
- 400g can chopped tomatoes
- 1 litre/1¾ pints chicken stock
- 50g/2oz roasted salted cashew nuts
- 1 small bunch coriander, leaves, chopped

1 Heat the oil in a large pan, fry the onions for 5 minutes until golden and softened, then tip on to a plate. Add the chicken breasts, browning for a few minutes on each side, then stir in the balti paste, quinoa and onions. Sizzle for a few minutes, then pour in the tomatoes and stock, and give everything a good mix. Bubble for 25 minutes until the quinoa is tender and saucy.

2 Stir in the cashews and most of the coriander with some seasoning, then scatter over the rest of the coriander to serve.

*PER SERVING 527 kcals, protein 47g, carbs 45g, fat 19g, sat fat 3g, fibre 5g, sugar 14g, salt 1.83g*

# Spiced prawn & coconut pilaf

By cooking the rice separately, the pilaf has no chance of becoming too sticky.

🕐 45 minutes    📂 4

- 4 tbsp vegetable oil
- 1 tsp cumin seeds
- 1 cinnamon stick
- 3 each whole cloves and cardamom pods
- 1 onion, finely sliced
- a fingertip-sized knob ginger, roughly chopped
- 2 large garlic cloves, sliced
- 2 tomatoes, quartered
- ½ tsp turmeric powder
- ¼ tsp hot chilli powder
- 1 heaped tsp ground coriander
- 300g/10oz raw peeled prawns
- 250g/9oz basmati rice, cooked according to pack instructions
- handful flaked coconut, to garnish (optional)

1 Heat the oil in a large non-stick pan, add the whole spices and, once they are sizzling, follow with the onion, frying for about 10 minutes until soft.

2 Meanwhile, make a paste using the ginger, garlic and tomatoes in a food processor. Add to the onion along with the remaining ground spices and cook over a low heat, stirring every now and then for 15 minutes.

3 Add the prawns and cook for a couple of minutes until pink. Stir in the cooked rice with a fork, heat through and serve scattered with the coconut, if using.

*PER SERVING 417 kcals, protein 19g, carbs 60g, fat 13g, sat fat 2g, fibre 1g, sugar 3g, salt 0.42g*

# Chilli-chicken curry

Serve with basmati rice cooked with cardamom pods, cloves and a cinnamon stick.

🕐 1 hour  🥘 4

- 1 medium onion, roughly chopped
- ½ x finger-length knob ginger, roughly chopped
- 2 garlic cloves, roughly chopped
- 1 tsp cumin seeds
- 2 tbsp vegetable oil
- ½ tsp each ground turmeric and hot chilli powder
- ½ x 400g can chopped tomatoes
- 350g/12oz potatoes, peeled and cut into chunks
- 500g/1lb 2oz bonless skinless chicken breasts, cut into chunks
- ½ tsp garam masala
- 2 tbsp chopped coriander leaves, to garnish
- cooked flavoured rice (see intro above) and natural yogurt, to serve

1 Blitz the onion, ginger and garlic in a food processor with 1 tablespoon water until smooth.
2 Fry the cumin seeds in the oil for a few seconds, then add the onion paste to soften for 5 minutes – splashing in a little water, if it starts to catch. Sprinkle in the turmeric and chilli. Add the tomatoes and fry for 5 minutes. Stir in the potatoes and 225ml/8fl oz hot water. Cook, covered, for 10 minutes.
3 Add the chicken and garam masala. Simmer for 15–20 minutes until cooked. Season, scatter over the coriander and serve with rice and natural yogurt.

. . . . . . . . . . . . . . . . . . . . . . . .
*PER SERVING 283 kcals, protein 34g, carbs 21g, fat 8g, sat fat 1g, fibre 2g, sugar none, salt 0.35g*

# All-in-one posh lamb balti

Feed a crowd with this gorgeous slow-cooked curry made from tender lamb shanks. Serve with cooling yogurt or raita, your favourite Indian pickles and plenty of rice.

 4 hours 55 minutes 🥧 5

- 5 lamb shanks
- 3–4 onions, halved and sliced
- 100g/4oz ginger, peeled and roughly chopped
- 6 garlic cloves
- 2 x 400g cans chopped tomatoes
- 6 tbsp balti paste
- 2 tbsp garam masala
- 4 tsp brown sugar
- handful each pomegranate seeds and coriander leaves, to garnish

**FOR THE MARINADE**

- 2 tbsp balti paste
- 2 tbsp sunflower or vegetable oil
- juice 1 lemon
- 2 tsp ground cumin
- 2 tsp brown mustard seeds
- 2 tsp ground turmeric
- 2 tsp kalonji seeds
- 1 tsp ground cinnamon

1 The day before, mix all the marinade ingredients together. Put the lamb shanks in a roasting tin and rub the marinade all over them. Cover and chill overnight.

2 Heat oven to 220C/200C fan/gas 7. Roast the lamb for 20 minutes to brown, then reduce the oven to 160C/140C fan/gas 3. Cover the tin tightly with a couple of layers of foil, so that no steam escapes, and return to the oven for another 3 hours.

3 Uncover the lamb and increase oven to 180C/160C fan/gas 4. Scatter the onions into the juices in the tin; roast for 30 minutes, uncovered. Meanwhile, whizz the ginger, garlic, 1 of the cans of chopped tomatoes, the balti paste, garam masala and sugar with a hand-held blender or in a food processor until fairly smooth. When the onions have cooked for 30 minutes, stir in the tomatoey paste with the second can of tomatoes. Return to the oven for 30 minutes.

4 Scatter the lamb with the pomegranate seeds and coriander, and serve.

*PER SERVING 670 kcals, protein 64g, carbs 19g, fat 39g, sat fat 15g, fibre 4g, sugar 13g, salt 1.2g*

# Red prawns with chilli & lime leaf

For a Thai-themed evening, serve this alongside a creamy green chicken curry, some jasmine rice and a crunchy salad (like the one on page 150).

🕐 20 minutes  🥧 6

- 3 long dried red chillies, deseeded and roughly chopped
- ½ tsp each coriander and cumin seeds
- 4 garlic cloves, finely chopped
- 1 lemongrass stalk, chopped
- 2 tbsp chopped coriander stalks
- 6 kaffir lime leaves, 3 finely shredded
- fingertip-sized knob ginger, chopped
- 2 tsp shrimp paste
- 3 tbsp oil
- 400g/14oz large raw peeled prawns, deveined
- 1½ tbsp each Thai fish sauce, caster sugar and lemon juice
- jasmine rice, to serve

1 To make the red curry paste, put the dried chillies, coriander and cumin seeds, 1 teaspoon of the chopped garlic, the lemongrass, coriander stalks, whole lime leaves, ginger and shrimp paste into a food processor, and whizz to a paste.

2 In a wok or frying pan, heat the oil and fry the remaining garlic until golden. Stir in the red curry paste and cook together for a few seconds. Add 3 tablespoons water and mix thoroughly. Tip in the prawns and cook for a few seconds over a high heat until evenly pink.

3 Stirring quickly after each addition, add the fish sauce, sugar, lemon juice and shredded lime leaves. Stir thoroughly for 2–3 seconds then serve with some jasmine rice.

*PER SERVING 146 kcals, protein 13g, carbs 6g, fat 8g, sat fat 1g, fibre trace, sugar 4g, salt 1.41g*

# Spicy lamb & squash supper

Sit this warming pot in the middle of the table and let everyone help themselves.

 1 hour  4

- 2 tbsp sunflower oil
- 1 onion, chopped
- 450g/1lb lamb fillet, cut into small pieces
- 1 garlic clove, chopped
- 2 tsp each ground cumin, ground coriander and hot chilli powder
- 1 small butternut squash, peeled and cut into small chunks
- 400g can chopped tomatoes
- 850ml/1½ pints lamb stock
- 50g/2oz red split lentils
- 3 tbsp chopped coriander leaves

1 Heat the oil in a large pan and fry the onion for about 4 minutes until golden. Stir in the lamb and garlic, and fry over a high heat for 3–4 minutes, stirring, until the lamb starts to brown. Add the spices and cook for 30 seconds, stirring constantly. Stir in the squash chunks.

2 Pour in the tomatoes and stock, add the lentils and bring to the boil. Simmer, partially covered, for about 30 minutes until the lamb and squash are tender. Season and stir in the coriander just before serving, reserving a little to sprinkle over the top.

*PER SERVING 459 kcals, protein 26g, carbs 31g, fat 27g, sat fat 11g, fibre 4g, sugar none, salt 1g*

# Tamarind fish curry

Tamarind is a sweet–sour paste often used in Indian cooking – you'll find it in small jars near the spices in the supermarket.

🕐 45 minutes   🄑 6

- 700g/1lb 9oz white fish fillets, skinned and cut into chunks
- 2 tbsp tamarind paste
- 2 tbsp vegetable oil
- 1 tsp mustard seeds
- 1 small onion, chopped
- 2 tbsp chopped ginger
- 2 plump garlic cloves, finely chopped
- ½ tsp ground turmeric
- 8 curry leaves (optional)
- 2 small green chillies, deseeded and thinly sliced
- 1 tsp ground coriander
- ¼ tsp ground cinnamon
- 150ml/¼ pint coconut milk
- 1 tsp malt vinegar
- rice, to serve

1 Pat dry the fish with kitchen paper. Dissolve the tamarind paste in a shallow bowl in 150ml/¼ pint water, then add the fish to the tamarind water for 15 minutes.

2 Meanwhile, heat the oil in a wok or frying pan. Fry the mustard seeds until crackling then stir in the onion and fry until brown. Add the ginger and garlic, and cook for 2 minutes, then the turmeric, curry leaves (if using), chillies, coriander and cinnamon, and stir for 1–2 minutes more. Add the coconut milk for 3–4 minutes.

3 Lift the fish out of the tamarind water, then add the water and the vinegar to the wok or pan, and bring to the boil. Put in the fish, lower the heat and simmer for 5 minutes until the fish is just cooked. Serve with rice.

*PER SERVING 196 kcals, protein 23g, carbs 6g, fat 9g, sat fat 4g, fibre trace, sugar 5g, salt 0.27g*

# Goan pork curry

In Goan cuisine, vinegar is often mixed with spices, giving a hot sharpness that cuts through rich meats such as pork belly.

 2½ hours, plus marinating   8

- 1.8kg/4lb pork belly, skinned and cut into large cubes
- 200ml/7fl oz white wine vinegar
- 1 tbsp hot chilli powder
- 3 tsp ground turmeric
- 2 tsp yellow mustard seeds
- 4 tsp cumin seeds
- sunflower oil, for frying
- 7 onions, 6 chopped and 1 sliced
- 8 garlic cloves, crushed
- thumb-sized knob ginger, grated
- chutney and naan bread, to serve

1 Put the meat in a large non-metallic bowl with the vinegar and spices. Mix well, cover and chill for up to 24 hours.

2 Heat 3 tablespoons of the oil in a deep frying pan, then fry the chopped onions, the garlic and ginger for 10 minutes until softened. Tip in the meat and all of the marinade, season, then let the meat cook in its own juices for about 10 minutes – it doesn't need to brown. Pour in enough water to cover, then simmer for about 1½ hours until the meat is very tender.

3 Meanwhile, heat 1cm/½in of the oil in a frying pan until hot, then fry the sliced onion for 4 minutes or until crisp and golden. Drain on kitchen paper, then sprinkle over the curry to serve, along with chutney and naan.

*PER SERVING 695 kcals, protein 46g, carbs 13g, fat 51g, sat fat 19g, fibre 2g, sugar 6g, salt 0.51g*

# Chicken curry with lime leaves, lemongrass & mango

Use a fragrant paste as the base for this Asian curry laced with tropical fruit and citrusy notes.

🕐 1 hour 10 minutes   📋 4

**FOR THE CURRY PASTE**
- 1 thumb-sized red chilli
- small pack coriander
- 6 lime leaves (2 finely chopped and the centre vein discarded)
- 6 lemongrass stalks, tough outer leaves removed, finely chopped
- 2.5cm/1in knob ginger, peeled
- 2 tbsp soft brown sugar
- 3 tbsp tamarind purée

**FOR THE CURRY**
- 2 tsp vegetable oil
- 400ml can coconut milk
- 8 boneless skinless chicken thighs, halved
- zest and juice 2 limes
- 100g/4oz fine green beans
- 2 small mangoes, peeled and cut into 2.5cm/1in pieces
- jasmine rice, to serve

1 Deseed the chilli for the curry paste (if you prefer). Remove the leaves of the coriander and reserve to garnish, then blend the stems in a food processor with the chilli and the rest of the curry-paste ingredients.

2 Heat the oil for the curry in a large pan, add the curry paste and cook on a medium heat for 2–3 minutes. Pour in the coconut milk and bring to a simmer. Add the chicken, lime zest and juice, then season and cover. Gently simmer for 30 minutes until the chicken is tender.

3 Remove the lid and cook for a further 10 minutes. Add the green beans, mangoes and whole lime leaves, and cook for 5 minutes. Add the coriander leaves just before serving with hot jasmine rice.

. . . . . . . . . . . . . . . . . . . . . . .
*PER SERVING 542 kcals, protein 35g, carbs 30g, fat 32g, sat fat 19g, fibre 2g, sugar 27g, salt 0.1g*

# Saffron-scented chicken

In India saffron is known as the royal spice and adds a sense of celebration and indulgence to food, which makes this dish ideal for serving at Diwali.

🕐 50 minutes    🍽 6

- 1 tbsp vegetable oil
- 1 tsp fennel seeds
- 2 garlic cloves, finely sliced
- 2 small onions, finely chopped
- 6 boneless skinless chicken breasts, each halved diagonally
- 4 tbsp korma curry paste
- a few saffron threads, plus extra to garnish
- 6 tbsp double cream
- 150g pot natural yogurt
- 1½ tsp clear honey
- handful sliced toasted almonds, to garnish
- hot naan bread, to serve

1 Heat the oil in a pan and add the fennel seeds. When the seeds begin to sizzle, add the garlic and onions. Sprinkle in some water, then cook for 5–8 minutes, or until golden.

2 Add the chicken to the pan and seal quickly. Add the korma paste and stir for 2 minutes. Add the saffron and 200ml/7fl oz water, cover, then simmer for 10–15 minutes to cook the chicken through completely.

3 Stir in the cream, yogurt and honey, and leave to cook for 3–5 minutes more. Serve topped with almonds, a few extra strands of saffron and some hot naan bread.

# Fragrant vegetable & cashew biryani

The korma paste used in this biryani adds its flavours of coconut, ginger, coriander and turmeric to the dish.

🕐 2 hours    🥧 8

- 8 tbsp sunflower oil
- 4 onions, halved and thinly sliced
- thumb-sized knob ginger, shredded
- 5 tbsp korma curry paste
- 2 cinnamon sticks
- 6 green cardamom pods
- 3 star anise
- 800g/1lb 12oz mix diced potato, cauliflower florets and frozen peas
- 250g/9oz Greek yogurt
- ½ tsp each rose water and ground turmeric
- 500g pack basmati rice, covered with water and soaked for 30 minutes
- 100g/4oz roasted salted cashew nuts
- handful coriander leaves

1 Heat 4 tablespoons of the oil and soften half of the onions. Add the ginger, curry paste, whole spices, potato and cauliflower for 1 minute, then add 300ml/½ pint water, cover and cook for 6 minutes. Stir in the peas, yogurt and 1 teaspoon salt.

2 In a bowl, mix together the rose water, turmeric and 3 tablespoons water. Drain the rice, boil in a pan of water for 5 minutes, then drain again.

3 Heat oven to 180C/160C fan/gas 4. Oil a large ovenproof dish with a lid. Layer in the veg sauce, nuts and rice, then drizzle over the rose-water mix. Cover with foil first, then the lid, and bake for 45 minutes–1 hour until hot through. To garnish, fry the remaining onions in the rest of the oil and add to the biryani with the coriander.

*PER SERVING 469 kcals, protein 14g, carbs 67g, fat 18g, sat fat 4g, fibre 4g, sugar 7g, salt 1.11g*

# Spicy lamb

Serve this delicious dish with warm naans to mop up the sauce. If you buy mini naans you can pop them in the toaster to heat, freeing up your oven if you're entertaining.

🕐 2 hours 20 minutes   🥧 8

- thumb-sized knob ginger, roughly chopped
- 2 onions, quartered
- 8 garlic cloves
- 2 mild red chillies, trimmed (and deseeded, if you like a milder flavour)
- 1 large bunch coriander
- 2 tbsp each fennel seeds, ground coriander and ground cumin
- 1.6kg/3lb 8oz diced lamb leg
- 2 tbsp olive oil
- 2 x 400g cans chopped tomatoes
- 2 tbsp tomato purée
- 300ml/½ pint lamb or vegetable stock
- 200g/8oz frozen peas
- handful chopped mint leaves

1 Put the ginger, onions, garlic, chillies and two-thirds of the coriander into a food processor and whizz to a coarse paste. Toss the fennel seeds, ground coriander and cumin with the lamb to coat.

2 Heat the oil in a large heavy-based pan and fry the lamb in batches for 4–5 minutes until well browned. Return all the meat to the pan, stir in the paste and fry for 8–10 minutes, stirring occasionally. Add the tomatoes, tomato purée and stock. Bring to the boil, cover and simmer gently for 1½ hours until the meat is tender.

3 Stir in the peas and some seasoning, and simmer gently for 3–4 minutes. Chop the remaining coriander, and scatter over with the chopped mint to serve.

*PER SERVING 485 kcals, protein 44g, carbs 12g, fat 30g, sat fat 13g, fibre 3g, sugar 5g, salt 0.67g*

# Jerk-chicken curry with beans

For something different, try this Caribbean curry. Serve with coconut rice, buttered corn cobs and lime wedges.

⏱ 50 minutes  🍽 4

- 8 chicken drumsticks or thighs
- 2 tbsp jerk seasoning
- 4 tsp olive oil
- 2 red onions, sliced
- 1 small bunch coriander, stalks finely chopped, leaves reserved
- 2 x 400g cans chopped tomatoes
- 410g can kidney beans, drained and rinsed

1 Toss the chicken in half the jerk seasoning and a little salt and black pepper. Heat half the oil in a large frying pan, quickly brown the chicken, then remove. Tip in the remaining oil, onions and coriander stalks, then soften for 5 minutes, stirring in the remaining jerk seasoning for the final minute.

2 Return the drumsticks or thighs to the pan, pour over the tomatoes, then bring to a simmer. Cover, then cook for 30 minutes. Remove the lid, stir in the beans, then cook for a further 10–15 minutes until the chicken is tender. Scatter with the coriander leaves and serve.

*PER SERVING 438 kcals, protein 45g, carbs 23g, fat 19g, sat fat 5g, fibre 7g, sugar 9g, salt 1.68g*

# Lamb, coconut & mango pilaf

This colourful one-pan dish is made for entertaining – try it with beef too.

 2 hours  6

- 1 tbsp sunflower oil
- 600g/1lb 5oz lamb shoulder, cut into large cubes
- 2 onions, sliced
- 2 garlic cloves, sliced
- 3 tbsp medium curry powder
- 1 fat red chilli, deseeded and thickly sliced
- 400ml can reduced-fat coconut milk
- 700ml/1¼ pints hot lamb stock
- 400g/14oz basmati rice
- 1 medium mango, peeled, stoned and sliced, plus a handful each chopped coriander and toasted flaked almonds, to garnish
- poppadoms, to serve

1 Heat oven to 180C/160C fan/gas 4. Heat the oil in a large, shallow ovenproof pan, tip in the lamb, then fry for 5 minutes until browned all over. Remove from the pan to a plate. Add the onions to the pan and fry until soft and golden. Tip in the garlic and curry powder, and fry for 1 minute more.

2 Stir the lamb back in with the chilli, coconut milk and stock, then bring to the boil. Cover and bake for 1 hour, until the lamb is tender.

3 Season, stir in the rice, re-cover pan, then return to oven for 30 minutes until liquid has been absorbed. Stand, covered, for 10 minutes, then fluff the rice with a fork. Scatter with the sliced mango, chopped coriander and toasted almonds, then serve straight from the pan with some poppadoms, if you like.

*PER SERVING 575 kcals, protein 27g, carbs 67g, fat 24g, sat fat 13g, fibre 4g, sugar none, salt 0.82g*

# Cumin-spiced chicken with tomatoes

Chicken thighs have a wonderful flavour when slow-cooked.

🕐 1¼ hours    🍽 4

- 4 tsp cumin seeds
- 3 tbsp vegetable oil
- 2 onions, diced
- 700g/1lb 9oz skinless chicken thighs
- 3 garlic cloves, chopped
- ½ x finger-length knob ginger, cut into thin sticks
- 400g can chopped tomatoes
- ¼ tsp ground turmeric
- ½ tsp chilli powder
- 2 tsp garam masala
- 3 tbsp chopped coriander leaves

1 Dry-roast 2 teaspoons of the cumin seeds in a pan for a few minutes. Set aside.
2 Heat the oil in a wok or frying pan and add the remaining cumin seeds. When the seeds are crackling, add the onions and fry until softened. Add the chicken for 5 minutes to seal, then add the garlic and ginger for 3–4 minutes more. Stir in the tomatoes, turmeric, chilli, garam masala, 2 tablespoons of the coriander leaves and 1 teaspoon salt, then cover and simmer for 45 minutes until the chicken is tender and the sauce is thick – if it is too runny, remove the lid and cook to reduce.
3 Coarsely grind the roasted cumin seeds and sprinkle over the dish with the remaining coriander leaves. Remove from the heat and cover for 5 minutes before serving.

*PER SERVING 320 kcals, protein 36g, carbs 12g, fat 14g, sat fat 3g, fibre 2g, sugar none, salt 1.86g*

# Winter-vegetable curry

Use hardy root veg in this Asian-inspired spice-pot. We used pumpkin, carrots and parsnips, teamed with juicy tomatoes.

🕐 1 hour 20 minutes   🥧 4

- 2 tbsp vegetable oil
- 2 onions, thinly sliced
- ½ pumpkin, winter squash or butternut squash, peeled, deseeded and cut into cubes
- 4 carrots, cut into batons
- 2 parsnips, cut into batons
- 3 tbsp curry paste
- 8 large ripe tomatoes, 2 cut into wedges
- 6 garlic cloves, peeled
- thumb-sized knob ginger, peeled and chopped
- small pack coriander, chopped
- small pack toasted flaked almonds
- rice and natural yogurt, to serve

1 Heat the oil in a large lidded pan. Tip in the onions and cook for 10 minutes until soft. Stir in the pumpkin or squash, carrots and parsnips, and cook for 5 minutes until they begin to soften. Add the curry paste and cook for another 3 minutes.

2 In a bowl, whizz together the whole tomatoes, garlic and ginger until smooth, then pour the tomato paste over the vegetables, adding 200ml/7fl oz water. Save a handful of coriander to garnish, and stir in the rest. Pop on the lid and simmer for 40 minutes or until the vegetables are tender. Uncover, stir through the tomato wedges and reduce to thicken the sauce.

3 Scatter the curry with the remaining coriander and the almonds. Season, then serve with rice and yogurt.

*PER SERVING 467 kcals, protein 13g, carbs 73g, fat 13g, sat fat 2g, fibre 12g, sugar 31g, salt 0.8g*

# Green chicken curry with aubergine

The leftover paste can be frozen for 3 months – add it to any recipe that calls for Thai green curry paste – or if time is short you can just use a shop-bought jar.

🕐 25 minutes  🍲 6

- 6 kaffir lime leaves, 3 finely shredded
- 1 tbsp vegetable oil
- 400ml can coconut milk
- 1 tbsp Thai fish sauce
- 1 tsp each caster sugar and lime juice
- 450g/1lb boneless skinless chicken breast
- 1 large or 6 baby aubergines
- 15 Thai basil leaves (optional)

**FOR THE GREEN CURRY PASTE**
- 3 green chillies, trimmed
- 1 lemongrass stalk
- 3 shallots, roughly chopped
- 3 garlic cloves
- ½ x finger-length knob ginger, chopped
- 3 tbsp chopped coriander stalks
- 1 tsp each ground coriander, ground cumin and shrimp paste

1 Put all the paste ingredients plus the whole lime leaves in a food processor and whizz to a paste.
2 In a wok or a large frying pan, heat the oil until very hot, then add 3 tablespoons of the curry paste and fry for a few seconds. Pour in the coconut milk, 100ml/3½fl oz water, the fish sauce, sugar and lime juice, then cover and simmer for 10 minutes. Cut the chicken and aubergines into bite-sized pieces, add to the pan and simmer gently for 8 minutes until both are cooked through. Stir in salt to taste, the shredded lime leaves and the basil leaves, if using, and serve.

*PER SERVING 236 kcals, protein 21g, carbs 6g, fat 15g, sat fat 10g, fibre 1g, sugar 4g, salt 0.97g*

# Goan prawn & coconut curry

Spice up your midweek meals with this curry in a hurry – throw a handful of spices in with shellfish, tomatoes and spinach.

🕐 30 minutes   🥧 2

- 1 tbsp sunflower oil
- 1 onion, thinly sliced
- 1 tbsp grated ginger
- 2 garlic cloves, crushed
- 1 red chilli, deseeded and sliced
- ½ tsp ground turmeric
- ½ tsp chilli powder
- 1 tsp ground coriander
- 10 fresh curry leaves
- 1 large potato, diced
- 400ml can half-fat coconut milk
- 8 cherry tomatoes, halved
- handful baby leaf spinach
- 200g/8oz raw peeled prawns
- rice, to serve

1 Heat the oil and fry the onion, ginger, garlic and chilli for 5 minutes until starting to soften. Add the spices, curry leaves and potato, then cook for 1 minute more. Stir in the coconut milk and tomatoes, cover and leave to simmer for 10 minutes until the potato is tender.

2 Add the spinach and prawns. Cook for 1 minute more until the spinach wilts and the prawns turn pink. Serve with rice.

*PER SERVING 417 kcals, protein 24g, carbs 30g, fat 21g, sat fat 13g, fibre 5g, sugar 9g, salt 0.6g*

# Aubergine curry with lemongrass & coconut milk

If you're making this for vegetarians, leave out the fish sauce and splash in a little light soy sauce instead.

🕐 40 minutes    🥧 4

- 3 large red chillies, deseeded and chopped
- 6 garlic cloves, roughly chopped
- knob ginger, chopped
- 2 lemongrass stalks, chopped
- 2 tbsp ground turmeric
- 1 tsp chilli powder
- 3 aubergines, quartered lengthways, then halved
- 1 tbsp olive oil
- 1 tbsp sugar
- 6 shallots, finely chopped
- 1 tbsp Thai fish sauce
- 400ml can coconut milk
- 400ml/14fl oz vegetable stock
- 1 small bunch coriander leaves, roughly chopped, to garnish
- jasmine rice or naan bread, to serve

1 In a food processor, pulse the chillies, garlic, ginger and lemongrass to a paste. Mix the turmeric and chilli powder together, and rub all over the aubergine wedges.

2 Heat the oil in a frying pan, brown the aubergines, then remove to a plate. Cook the paste, sugar and shallots for a few minutes, then return the aubergines to the pan. Add the fish sauce, coconut milk and stock, and bring to the boil. Reduce the heat and cook gently until the aubergine is tender, but not mushy, about 15 minutes. Season, sprinkle with the coriander and serve with steamed rice or warm naan bread to mop up the sauce.

*PER SERVING 268 kcals, protein 5g, carbs 17g, fat 20g, sat fat 14g, fibre 3g, sugar 10g, salt 1.39g*

# Black-pepper chicken

This is a light curry that provides balance alongside richer dishes.

 1 hour, plus marinating   6

- 175g/6oz natural yogurt
- 1 small bunch coriander, leaves chopped
- 2 tbsp black peppercorns, coarsely crushed
- 2 tbsp grated ginger
- 2 tbsp crushed garlic
- 1 tbsp lemon juice
- 900g/2lb boneless skinless chicken breasts, cut into large chunks
- 4 tbsp vegetable oil
- 1 large onion, chopped
- 1 tsp garam masala
- 1 large tomato, chopped

1 In a bowl, mix together the yogurt, coriander, peppercorns, half the ginger, half the garlic, the lemon juice and some salt. Stir in the chicken and leave to marinate for 1 hour.

2 Heat the oil in a wok or a wide pan, then fry the onion until browned. Stir in the masala, remaining ginger and garlic and the chopped tomato, then reduce the heat and cook for 10–15 minutes, uncovered, stirring occasionally.

3 Add the chicken and marinade to the pan. Pour in 75–100ml/2½–3½fl oz water, or enough to make a thickish sauce. Bring to the boil, cover and simmer gently for 25 minutes, stirring occasionally, until the chicken is cooked through.

*PER SERVING 175 kcals, protein 39g, carbs 10g, fat 10g, sat fat 2g, fibre 1g, sugar 5g, salt 0.3g*

# Lamb, chickpea & spinach curry with masala mash

· · · · · · · · · · · · · · · · · · · · · ·

OK, so it isn't authentic, but a fragrant mash is ideal for mopping up curry sauces.

🕐 1¾ hours    🥧 4

- 1 tbsp oil
- 500g/1lb 2oz lean lamb leg, cubed
- 1 red onion, sliced
- fingertip-sized knob ginger, finely chopped
- 2 garlic cloves, crushed
- 1 tbsp each ground cumin and ground coriander
- 400g can chopped tomatoes
- ½ x 410g can chickpeas, drained and rinsed
- 1 tsp garam masala
- 100g/4oz spinach leaves, roughly chopped
- 700g/1lb 9oz potatoes, peeled and quartered
- 1 tbsp korma curry paste
- 100g/3½oz thick natural yogurt

1 Heat the oil in a large frying pan, brown the lamb thoroughly then remove to a plate. Add the onion and cook until golden brown, then stir in the ginger, garlic, cumin and coriander, and cook for 2 minutes more until fragrant. Return the lamb to the pan, add the tomatoes, bring to the boil, then simmer gently for 1½ hours until the meat is really tender. (Add splashes of water if the sauce becomes too dry.) Add the chickpeas and garam masala then simmer for 5 minutes more. Stir through the spinach to wilt, then season.

2 Meanwhile, boil the potatoes until soft, about 15 minutes. Drain and mash with the curry paste and yogurt. Serve with the curry.

· · · · · · · · · · · · · · · · · · · · · · · · ·
*PER SERVING 469 kcals, protein 38g, carbs 48g, fat 15g, sat fat 5g, fibre 6g, sugar none, salt 1.04g*

# Pumpkin curry with chickpeas

This is a delicious curry by itself, or served as an accompaniment to a spicy roasted chicken or leg of lamb.

🕐 40 minutes  🥧 4

- 1 tbsp sunflower oil
- 3 tbsp Thai yellow curry paste
- 2 onions, finely chopped
- 3 large lemongrass stalks, bashed
- 6 cardamom pods
- 1 tbsp mustard seeds
- 1kg/2lb 4oz butternut squash, peeled, deseeded and cut into chunks
- 400ml/14fl oz vegetable stock
- 400ml can reduced-fat coconut milk
- 410g can chickpeas, drained and rinsed
- 2 limes
- large handful mint leaves, to garnish
- naan bread, to serve

1 Heat the oil in a deep frying pan, then gently fry the paste, onions, lemongrass, cardamom pods and mustard seeds for 2–3 minutes until fragrant. Stir in the squash for a few minutes, then pour in the stock and coconut milk. Bring to a simmer and cook for 20 minutes, then add the chickpeas for another 10 minutes until the squash is tender.

2 Squeeze the juice of 1 of the limes into the curry, then cut the other into wedges. Tear over the mint leaves, then serve with lime wedges to squeeze over and some naan bread.

*PER SERVING 293 kcals, protein 9g, carbs 26g, fat 18g, sat fat 10g, fibre 7g, sugar 10g, salt 1.3g*

# Coriander, tomato & mango dips with poppadums

• • • • • • • • • • • • • • • • • • • • • •

Keep dinner guests happy nibbling on these while you finish preparing the main course.

🕐 30 minutes  🥘 8

• mango chutney and poppadums, to serve (optional)

**FOR THE CREAMY CORIANDER**

• ½ x thumb-sized knob ginger, roughly chopped
• 2 garlic cloves
• ½ small bunch coriander, leaves only
• ½ mild red chilli, deseeded and finely chopped
• 300g/10oz natural yogurt

**FOR THE CHUNKY TOMATO**

• 4 tomatoes, finely chopped
• 1 small red onion, finely chopped
• 2 tsp kalonji seeds
• juice 1 lime
• 1 tbsp chopped coriander

1 For the creamy coriander dip, whizz the ginger, garlic, coriander and most of the chilli to a paste in a food processor. Stir with the yogurt and chill until ready to serve.

2 For the tomato dip, combine the chopped tomatoes, onion, kalonji seeds, lime juice and coriander with some seasoning.

3 To serve, scatter the coriander dip with remaining chilli, scrape the mango chutney into a bowl, and transfer the chunky tomato dip to a serving bowl. Eat with poppadums, if you like.

• • • • • • • • • • • • • • • • • • • • • •

*PER SERVING 46 kcals, protein 3g, carbs 6g, fat 2g, sat fat 1g, fibre 1g, sugar 5g, salt 0.09g*

# Spicy Indian rice

This golden rice will work with almost any Indian curry.

🕐 30 minutes   🥘 4

- 2 onions, sliced
- 2 tbsp sunflower oil
- ½ tsp ground turmeric
- 1 cinnamon stick
- mugful long grain rice
- 6 cardamom pods, bashed with a rolling pin
- 1 tsp cumin seeds
- large handful sultanas
- large handful roasted cashew nuts

1 Fry the onions in the oil in a large frying pan for 10–12 minutes until golden. Set aside.

2 Fill a big pan with water, bring to the boil and tip in a heaped teaspoon of salt – the water will bubble furiously. Add the turmeric, cinnamon stick and rice. Stir once and return to the boil, then turn the heat down a little so that the water is boiling steadily, but not vigorously. Boil uncovered, without stirring, for 10 minutes until the rice is tender but with a little bite. Drain in a large sieve and rinse by pouring over a kettle of boiling water.

3 Stir the cardamom pods into the pan of onions with the cumin seeds, return to the heat and fry briefly. Toss in the sultanas and roasted cashew nuts, then the hot drained rice. Serve immediately.

*PER SERVING 449 kcals, protein 8g, carbs 82g, fat 12g, sat fat 2g, fibre 1g, sugar 13g, salt 0.03g*

# Thai cucumber salad with sour-chilli dressing

A sharp, fresh salad – ideal for serving alongside creamy Thai curries.

🕐 10 minutes   🥧 4

- 1 cucumber, cut into ribbons with a peeler
- 1 Little Gem lettuce, shredded
- 140g/5oz beansprouts
- 1 bunch coriander, leaves roughly chopped
- 1 bunch mint, leaves roughly chopped

**FOR THE DRESSING**
- 1 tsp rice wine vinegar
- 1 tbsp Thai fish sauce
- ½ tsp light muscovado sugar
- 2 red chillies, deseeded and finely chopped

1 Mix the dressing ingredients together, stirring until the sugar is dissolved, then set aside until ready to serve.
2 Put the salad ingredients in a bowl, then pour over the dressing, mixing well to combine. Serve immediately.

*PER SERVING 27 kcals, protein 2g, carbs 4g, fat 1g, sat fat none, fibre 1g, sugar 3g, salt 0.75g*

# Vegetables with Jaipuri spices

Jaipur is the capital of Rajasthan, where the food tends to be milder and subtly spiced.

🕐 1 hour    🍽 6

- 2 tbsp vegetable oil
- 1 tsp cumin seeds
- 2 small onions, chopped
- 2 tbsp rogan josh curry paste
- 200g/8oz potatoes, peeled and diced
- 5 tomatoes, roughly chopped
- 2 large carrots, peeled, halved and sliced lengthways
- 200g/8oz green beans, trimmed
- 200g/8oz peas, thawed if frozen
- 4 tbsp Greek yogurt
- 3 tbsp chopped coriander leaves
- juice ½ lemon

1 Heat the oil in a pan, then add the cumin seeds. When they sizzle, add the onions and cook for 5–8 minutes or until golden brown. Stir in the curry paste and 50ml/2fl oz water, then cook for 2 more minutes.

2 Mix in the potatoes, stir well, then tip in the tomatoes and 225ml/8fl oz water. Cover and cook for 10 minutes before adding the carrots for another 10 minutes. Stir occasionally to prevent the sauce sticking. Add the green beans for about 5 minutes more, then the peas, Greek yogurt and 2 tablespoons of the coriander. Leave to cook for 2 more minutes before checking the seasoning. Squeeze in the lemon juice and serve garnished with the remaining coriander.

*PER SERVING 138 kcals, protein 5g, carbs 14g, fat 8g, sat fat 2g, fibre 4g, sugar 7g, salt 0.31g*

# Honey-roasted swede with chilli & cumin

· · · · · · · · · · · · · · · · · · · · · ·

This versatile root vegetable can be roasted like a potato – with a drizzle of honey and a sprinkling of spice you get a very special side dish.

🕐 50 minutes   🥧 4

- 1 large swede, peeled and cut into large chunks
- 2 tbsp olive oil
- 1 tbsp clear honey
- 1 tsp cumin seeds
- 1 large red chilli, deseeded and chopped
- small bunch coriander leaves, chopped

1 Heat oven to 200C/180C fan/gas 6. Toss the swede in olive oil in a shallow roasting tin, then season. Roast in the oven for 35–40 minutes, tossing occasionally, until the swede is golden and soft.

2 Stir in the honey and cumin seeds, and continue to roast for 10 minutes until just starting to catch. Remove and stir through the chilli and coriander to serve.

· · · · · · · · · · · · · · · · · · · · · · · · ·
*PER SERVING 97 kcals, protein 1g, carbs 10g, fat 6g, sat fat 1g, fibre 3g, sugar 10g, salt 0.1g*

# Fresh mango relish

This sweet–sour relish makes a great accompaniment to some warm naan bread or a spicy curry.

 15 minutes    4–6

- 2 large ripe mangoes
- juice 1 lime
- 1 tbsp tamarind paste
- handful each mint and coriander leaves

1 Peel and stone both mangoes then finely dice two-thirds of the flesh. Tip into a small serving bowl.

2 Roughly chop the remaining flesh and whizz until smooth in a small food processor or with a hand-held blender with the lime juice and tamarind paste. Add the herbs and pulse for a second. Stir the mango sauce into the diced mango and chill for up to an hour before serving.

*PER SERVING (4) 68 kcals, protein 1g, carbs 17g, fat trace, sat fat none, fibre 3g, sugar none, salt 0.01g*

# Tomato, cucumber & coriander salad

· · · · · · · · · · · · · · · · · · · · · ·

Colourful and crunchy, this salad works well as part of a large spread and can be easily doubled to feed a crowd.

🕐 15 minutes    🥧 6    ◗ Easily doubled

- 6 vine tomatoes, chopped
- 1 small cucumber, diced
- 1 red onion, finely chopped
- 2 tbsp chopped coriander leaves

1 Mix together all of the salad ingredients and chill until needed.
2 About 15 minutes before you are ready to eat, remove the salad from the fridge and let it come to room temperature. Season just before serving (otherwise the salad can become watery).

· · · · · · · · · · · · · · · · · · · · · · ·
*PER SERVING 34 kcals, protein 2g, carbs 6g, fat none, sat fat none, fibre 2g, sugar 6g, salt 0.03g*

# Satay noodles with crunchy veg

A good midweek accompaniment to a quick Thai curry; you get your noodles and veg all in one.

🕐 15 minutes   🥧 4

- 3 tbsp crunchy peanut butter
- 3 tbsp sweet chilli sauce
- 2 tbsp soy sauce
- 300g pack straight-to-wok noodles
- 1 tbsp oil
- thumb-sized knob ginger, grated
- 300g pack stir-fry vegetables
- handful basil leaves
- 25g/1oz roasted peanuts, roughly chopped

1 Mix the peanut butter, chilli and soy sauces in a small bowl with 100ml/3½fl oz hot water to make a smooth satay sauce. Set aside.
2 Put the noodles in a bowl and pour boiling water over them. Stir gently to separate, then drain thoroughly.
3 Heat the oil in a wok, then stir-fry the ginger and harder pieces of veg from the stir-fry mix, such as peppers, for 2 minutes. Add the noodles and the rest of the veg, then stir-fry over a high heat for 1–2 minutes until the veg are just cooked.
4 Push the veg to one side of the pan, then pour the satay sauce into the other side, tilting the pan. Bring to the boil. Mix the sauce with the stir-fry, then sprinkle over the basil leaves and peanuts to serve.

*PER SERVING 286 kcals, protein 10g, carbs 34g, fat 14g, sat fat 2g, fibre 5g, sugar 6g, salt 2.29g*

# Coriander parathas

The parathas can be cooked several hours ahead then reheated in the oven, wrapped in foil, at 180C/160C fan/gas 4 for 10 minutes.

🕐 30 minutes    🍳 10

- 450g/1lb chapatti flour, plus extra for rolling
- 1 tsp salt
- 6 tbsp chopped coriander leaves
- 300ml/½ pint warm water
- oil, for brushing

1 Mix together the flour, salt and coriander. Gradually add the water, mixing to make a dough – it should be neither too sticky nor too dry or it will be difficult to roll. Cut into 10 balls and cover loosely with a tea towel.

2 Heat a cast-iron pan or griddle until hot. Lightly roll out each ball, sprinkling with a little flour to prevent sticking, into a 20cm/8in circle. Slap the paratha on to the dry pan or griddle and cook for 45 seconds–1 minute until it starts to puff, then turn over. Brush the cooked side with oil, turn over again and cook for 20 seconds. Brush the other side with oil, turn and cook for 20 seconds.

3 Remove the paratha to a plate and cover loosely with a tea towel. Repeat with the remaining dough until you have 10 parathas.

*PER PARATHA 187 kcals, protein 5g, carbs 37g, fat 3g, sat fat trace, fibre 2g, sugar 1g, salt 0.52g*

# Turmeric pilaf with golden onions

This pilaf can be made ahead – just cool it quickly by spreading on a baking sheet, then chill until needed. Reheat in a microwave until piping hot.

🕐 30 minutes   🍳 6

- 400g/14oz basmati rice
- 4 tbsp olive oil
- 1½ tsp cumin seeds
- 1 tsp black mustard seeds
- 2 large onions, halved and sliced
- just under 1 tsp ground turmeric
- 2 red or green chillies, deseeded and thinly sliced

1 Thoroughly rinse the rice until the water looks completely clear. Drain, then tip into a large pan of salted water. Bring to the boil and cook for 6 minutes until just tender. Drain well.

2 Heat the oil in a large wok and fry the seeds until they start to pop. Add the onions and cook, stirring frequently, until they are tender and golden. Stir in the turmeric and chillies, and cook for 1–2 minutes more. Add the rice and heat through, stirring, until thoroughly hot. Serve immediately.

*PER SERVING 323 kcals, protein 6g, carbs 60g, fat 8g, sat fat 1g, fibre 1g, sugar 4g, salt 0.01g*

# Coriander & mango raita

A cooling raita is the perfect match for a hot and spicy curry.

🕐 15 minutes   🍴 6

- 1 tsp cumin seeds
- 500g pot natural yogurt
- 3 tbsp chopped coriander leaves
- 1 ripe mango, peeled and diced
- finger-length piece cucumber, deseeded and chopped
- 1 green chilli, deseeded and finely chopped
- 1 tsp golden caster sugar

1 Dry-roast the cumin seeds in a pan on a low heat, moving them around. After a few minutes, they will begin to change colour to a golden brown. Remove from the heat and crush coarsely using a pestle and mortar.
2 Put all the other ingredients in a bowl and stir in the crushed seeds. Season with salt to taste.

*PER SERVING 83 kcals, protein 5g, carbs 14g, fat 1g, sat fat none, fibre 1g, sugar 14g, salt 0.14g*

# Spinach with coconut

The addition of fresh coconut makes this a typically southern Indian dish.

 45 minutes    6

- 50g/2oz yellow split peas or red split lentils
- 2 tbsp vegetable oil
- 1 tsp mustard seeds
- 5 curry leaves (optional)
- 2 small thin red chillies
- 1 small onion, chopped
- 250g/9oz spinach leaves, shredded
- ½ fresh coconut, flesh grated

1 In a pan of boiling water, cook the split peas for about 25 minutes until they are tender but still keep their shape. Or, if you are using lentils, cook them for 15–20 minutes.
2 Meanwhile, heat the vegetable oil in a large pan, then add the mustard seeds, curry leaves (if using), whole red chillies and chopped onion; fry for 5 minutes.
3 Wash and drain the shredded spinach. Drain the split peas or lentils, then add to the pan of spices with the grated coconut, and toss over the heat for another 5 minutes. Add the spinach and when it has wilted, season and serve.

*PER SERVING 136 kcals, protein 4g, carbs 6g, fat 11g, sat fat 6g, fibre 2g, sugar 2g, salt 0.16g*

# Prawn, mango & spring-onion pakoras

· · · · · · · · · · · · · · · · · · · ·

A pakora's characteristic crisp batter comes from the gram or chickpea flour with which it is made. Look for gram flour in Indian stores or health-food shops.

🕐 40 minutes   🥟 24

- 140g/5oz gram or plain flour
- 2 tsp garam masala
- 1 tsp ground turmeric
- 3 green chillies, deseeded and finely chopped
- 1 small mango, peeled and chopped
- 4 spring onions, finely sliced
- 200g/8oz raw peeled prawns, chopped
- vegetable oil, for deep-frying

**FOR THE DIP**
- 200ml carton coconut cream
- large knob ginger, roughly chopped
- handful coriander leaves

1 Heat the oven to its lowest temperature. Tip the flour into a large bowl and stir in the spices and a large pinch of salt. Make a well in the middle, then gradually whisk in 100ml/3½fl oz water until you have a smooth but thick batter. Mix in the chillies, mango, spring onions and prawns.

2 Heat 5cm/2in oil in a deep pan, then drop in spoonfuls of the mix. Fry four at a time for 3–4 minutes, until crisp and lightly golden. Drain on kitchen paper and keep warm in a low oven until ready to serve.

3 For the dip, blend the coconut cream, ginger and coriander together in a food processor until smooth. Serve in a bowl alongside the pakoras.

· · · · · · · · · · · · · · · · · · · · · · · · ·

*PER PAKORA 97 kcals, protein 3g, carbs 5g, fat 7g, sat fat 3g, fibre 1g, sugar 2g, salt 0.05g*

# Peppery fennel & carrot salad

This zingy, superhealthy salad will liven up any table.

 10 minutes  6

- 2 large carrots, cut into thin sticks or grated
- 2 large fennel bulbs, quartered and thinly sliced
- handful peanuts or cashew nuts, chopped
- 2 tbsp olive oil
- 1 tsp mustard seeds
- 1 tsp kalonji seeds
- juice 1 lemon or lime

1 Tip the carrots and fennel into a large salad bowl. Set aside.
2 Toast the nuts in a hot frying pan for 3–5 minutes until golden, then tip out on to a plate. In the same pan, heat the oil and fry the mustard and kalonji seeds until they begin to pop – about 30 seconds. Pour in the lemon or lime juice and mix together to make a dressing.
3 Toss the dressing with the vegetables in the bowl, then sprinkle with the nuts to serve.

*PER SERVING 87 kcals, protein 2g, carbs 6g, fat 6g, sat fat 1g, fibre 3g, sugar 5g, salt 0.05g*

# Green-apple salad

In Thailand green-mango salad is a popular dish, but green mangoes can be hard to find – here we've swapped them for crisp green apples instead.

🕐 15 minutes    🥧 4

- 2 shallots, finely sliced
- 1 tbsp vegetable oil
- 5 sharp green apples, such as Granny Smith, cored and thinly sliced
- 6 cherry tomatoes, quartered
- 2 tbsp dry-roasted peanuts, crushed
- handful coriander leaves, chopped

**FOR THE DRESSING**
- 1 garlic clove, finely chopped
- 1 red chilli, deseeded and finely chopped
- 1 tsp sugar
- 1 tbsp Thai fish sauce
- juice 2 limes

1 To make the dressing, whizz together the garlic, chilli, sugar, fish sauce and lime juice in a food processor. Set aside.
2 Fry the shallots in the oil for 5 minutes or until crisp and golden brown. Remove with a slotted spoon and drain on kitchen paper.
3 Toss the apples with the tomatoes and dressing. Spoon on to plates and top with the peanuts, crisp shallots and coriander.

*PER SERVING 152 kcals, protein 3g, carbs 21g, fat 7g, sat fat 1g, fibre 3g, sugar 1g, salt 0.9g*

# Sri Lankan runner-bean curry

Coconut milk not only cools down this vegan spice-pot but also allows the key flavours of the ginger, cinnamon, cloves, mustard seeds and garam masala to stand out.

🕐 30 minutes  🍕 4

- 1 small onion, roughly chopped
- ¼ tsp turmeric powder
- large knob ginger, peeled and roughly chopped
- 4 garlic cloves
- 2 tbsp vegetable oil
- 2 tsp black mustard seeds
- 5 fresh curry leaves
- 1 tbsp mild curry powder
- 400ml can coconut milk
- 4 whole cloves
- 1 cinnamon stick
- 1 whole dried red chilli
- 300g/10oz runner beans, stringed and sliced
- juice 1 lime
- 1 tsp garam masala
- handful coriander leaves
- rice and rotis, to serve (optional)

1 In a blender, combine the onion, turmeric, ginger, garlic and 1 tablespoon of the oil together with a large pinch of salt. Heat the remaining oil in a shallow pan. Add the mustard seeds and curry leaves, and cook until they crackle, then add the onion paste and cook until sticky.

2 Stir through the curry powder, then pour in the coconut milk. Add the cloves, cinnamon and the chilli, and bring to a simmer. Tip in the beans and simmer for 15 minutes or until tender. Squeeze in the lime juice, add the garam masala, take the pan off the heat and stir through the coriander. Serve with rice and rotis, if you like.

PER SERVING 267 kcals, protein 4g, carbs 9g, fat 25g, sat fat 16g, fibre 4g, sugar 4g, salt 0.2g

# Indian bread with courgettes & & coriander

This bread is called thepla in India; serve with small bowls of natural yogurt and mango chutney.

🕐 1 hour    🥧 12

- ½ tsp cumin seeds
- 450g/1lb courgettes, coarsely grated
- 175g/6oz plain flour, plus extra for rolling
- 175g/6oz plain wholemeal flour
- 2 tsp grated ginger
- good pinch turmeric powder
- small handful coriander leaves, chopped
- 3–4 tbsp sunflower oil

1 Dry-fry the cumin seeds for 1 minute in a non-stick pan until toasted.

2 Mix the toasted cumin seeds with the grated courgettes, flours, ginger, turmeric and coriander in a large bowl with 1 teaspoon salt. Rub in 1½ tablespoons of the oil, then slowly mix in 4–5 tablespoons cold water until a soft dough forms. Tear into 12 pieces and shape into balls.

3 Using a little extra flour, roll each piece into a thin 14cm/5½in round. Heat a griddle or heavy-based frying pan until very hot. Add one or two breads and cook for 2 minutes, patting with a clean cloth – this helps the bread cook fast. Turn the breads over and cook for around 2 minutes more.

4 Drizzle a little oil over, turn the breads again for 30–60 seconds more, then drizzle a few drops of oil on this side. Remove and repeat with the rest. Serve hot or cold.

*PER THEPLA 257 kcals, protein 8g, carbs 43g, fat 7g, sat fat 1g, fibre 4g, sugar none, salt 0.01g*

# Indian summer salad

An Indian-style coleslaw that's delicious served with tomato-based curries or spicy grilled meats.

🕐 20 minutes   🥧 6

- 3 carrots
- 1 bunch radishes
- 2 courgettes
- ½ small red onion
- small handful mint leaves

**FOR THE DRESSING**
- 1 tbsp white wine vinegar
- 1 tsp Dijon mustard
- 1 tbsp mayonnaise
- 2 tbsp olive oil

1 Grate the carrots into a large bowl. Thinly slice the radishes and courgettes, and finely chop the onion. Mix all the vegetables together in the bowl with the mint leaves.

2 Whisk together the vinegar, mustard and mayonnaise for the dressing until smooth, then gradually whisk in the oil. Add salt and freshly ground black pepper to taste, then drizzle over the salad and mix well before serving.

*PER SERVING 79 kcals, protein 1g, carbs 5g, fat 6g, sat fat 1g, fibre 2g, sugar 6g, salt 0.35g*

# Mango & cardamom ice cream

Kulfi, or Indian ice cream, is popular in northern India, but ice cream like this one here is popular throughout the southern regions.

🕐 1¼ hours, plus chilling and freezing    🥧 6

- 1.4 litres/2½ pints full-fat milk
- 200g/8oz golden caster sugar
- 1 tsp ground cardamom, or crushed seeds from about 30 pods
- 2 tbsp slivered pistachio nuts
- 1 tbsp desiccated coconut
- 1 medium mango, peeled and diced
- crushed cardamom seeds, mango slices and lime juice, to decorate

1 Put the milk and sugar in a pan, and bring to the boil for 15 minutes, stirring constantly to prevent it bubbling over. Lower the heat and simmer, uncovered, for 35–45 minutes, stirring occasionally, until reduced by half. Stir in the ground cardamom. Pour into a bowl and leave to cool to room temperature.

2 Churn the cooled cardamom milk in an ice-cream maker, stirring in the nuts, coconut and mango before transferring to six cups or moulds and freezing overnight. If you don't have an ice-cream maker, freeze the cooled milk for an hour until small crystals form, then stir in the bits and transfer to the individual cups or moulds for freezing.

3 About 5 minutes before serving, remove the cups or moulds from the freezer then turn out the ice cream on to six serving plates. Scatter over a little crushed cardamom and the mango slices, and a sprinkling of lime juice.

*PER SERVING 362 kcals, protein 9g, carbs 57g, fat 12g, sat fat 7g, fibre 2g, sugar 57g, salt 0.26g*

# Spiced & sweet lassis

· · · · · · · · · · · · · · · · · · ·

A lassi is a refreshing, non-alcoholic Indian drink.

 15 minutes, plus cooling      6

- 2 tbsp cumin seeds
- 2 tbsp rose water
- 85g/3oz caster sugar
- few coriander leaves
- 500g tub low-fat natural yogurt

1 Toast the cumin seeds in a non-stick frying pan for 1 minute, then set aside to cool.

2 In a small pan, mix the rose water and sugar with 50ml/2fl oz water. Heat gently until the sugar has melted, then bubble for a minute until syrupy. Cool.

3 To serve, put the rose water syrup, toasted cumin seeds and coriander leaves into three separate small serving bowls. Using a balloon whisk, whisk the yogurt with 450ml/16fl oz cold water until frothy. Divide among six tumblers and let everyone help themselves to either a sprinkling of cumin seeds and coriander (for a spiced lassi) or a drizzle of rose water syrup (for a sweet lassi).

· · · · · · · · · · · · · · · · · · · · · · ·   ᷐ ᷐

*PER SERVING (spiced) 115 kcals, protein 5g, carbs 22g, fat 2g, sat fat 1g, fibre none, sugar 20g, salt 0.18g • (sweet) 99 kcals, protein 4g, carbs 20g, fat 1g, sat fat 1g, fibre none, sugar 20g, salt 0.16g*

# Coconut-ice squares

Curries can be filling, so if you don't fancy finishing with a proper dessert just serve a few squares of this sweet treat.

🕐 15 minutes, plus 3 hours or overnight setting 　🥧 32

- 50g/2oz sweetened condensed milk
- 250g/9oz icing sugar, sifted, plus extra for dusting
- 200g/8oz desiccated coconut
- pink edible food colouring

1 Using a wooden spoon, mix together the condensed milk and icing sugar in a large bowl. It will get very stiff. Work the coconut into the mix until well combined – use your hands, if you like.

2 Split the mix into two and knead a very small amount of the food colouring into one half. Dust a board with extra icing sugar, then shape each half into a smooth rectangle and put one on top of the other. Roll with a rolling pin, re-shaping with your hands every couple of rolls, until you have a rectangle of two-tone coconut ice about 3cm/1¼in thick.

3 Transfer to a plate or board and leave, uncovered, for at least 3 hours (or ideally overnight) to set. Cut into 32 squares with a sharp knife and keep for up to a month in an airtight container.

*PER SQUARE 76 kcals, protein 1g, carbs 10g, fat 4g, sat fat 3g, fibre 1g, sugar 10g, salt 0.01g*

# Pineapple with chilli & vanilla syrup

· · · · · · · · · · · · · · · · · · · · ·

Instead of canned, you can use fresh fruit – slice into rings, remove the core and replace the syrup from the can with double the amount of sugar and water used here.

🕐 10 minutes   🥧 4

- 432g can pineapple rings in syrup
- 50g/2oz caster sugar
- 1 vanilla pod, split and seeds scraped out
- ½ red chilli, deseeded and thinly sliced
- 25g/1oz unsalted butter
- Greek yogurt or coconut ice cream, to serve

1 Drain the pineapple, reserving the syrup. Put the syrup, 3 tablespoons water, the sugar, vanilla pod and chilli in a small pan, and bring to the boil. Once the syrup has come to the boil, take off the heat and leave to infuse and cool.

2 Melt the butter in a non-stick pan. When the butter stops foaming and is about to turn brown, add the pineapple and brown on both sides.

3 Add the chilli syrup and bring to the boil. The butter will slightly thicken the syrup. Serve warm with Greek yogurt or coconut ice cream.

· · · · · · · · · · · · · · · · · · · · · · · · ·
*PER SERVING 166 kcals, protein 1g, carbs 31g, fat 5g, sat fat 3g, fibre 1g, sugar 31g, salt 0.01g*

# Fruity coconut creams

These little pots are just the right size for serving after an Indian spread.

🕙 10 minutes, plus chilling    4

- 50g sachet creamed coconut
- 500g tub 0% Greek yogurt
- 85g/3oz icing sugar, sifted
- few drops vanilla extract
- 2 kiwi fruits
- 400g can pineapple chunks in juice

1 Dissolve the sachet of creamed coconut in 50ml/2fl oz boiling water, then leave to cool. Spoon the yogurt into a mixing bowl, then stir in the icing sugar and vanilla. Combine the vanilla with the coconut mix, then spoon into four individual glasses. Chill until ready to serve.

2 Peel and chop the kiwi fruit into small pieces. Drain the pineapple, then chop the chunks into small pieces. Mix the fruit together, then spoon over the top of the coconut creams to serve.

*PER SERVING 266 kcals, protein 19g, carbs 40g, fat 5g, sat fat 4g, fibre 1g, sugar 39g, salt 0.16g*

# Poached aromatic fruits

. . . . . . . . . . . . . . . . . . . . . .

Desserts are rarely served in India, but this special pud often makes an appearance at Diwali celebrations.

🕐 35 minutes     🥧 6

- 2 oranges, peeled and segmented
- 2 pears, peeled, quartered lengthways and cored
- 100g/4oz dried figs
- 100g/4oz prunes
- 85g/3oz dried cranberries
- 140g/5oz caster sugar
- 4 whole cloves
- 3 cardamom pods
- 1 cinnamon stick
- few mint leaves, to decorate
- crème fraîche, to serve

1 Put the fresh and dried fruits in a pan with just enough water to cover. Add the sugar, cloves, cardamom pods and cinnamon stick. Bring to the boil, then reduce the heat and allow the fruits to cook gently for 10–15 minutes or until they are soft. Discard the whole spice, if you like.

2 Strain off the fruit, reserving the liquid in the pan, into a bowl. Put the cooking liquid back on a high heat and boil until thick and syrupy. Cool for use later or keep warm until just before serving.

3 Divide the fruit among six bowls and pour over some of the aromatic syrup. Top with mint leaves and serve with crème fraîche.

. . . . . . . . . . . . . . . . . . . . . . . .

*PER SERVING 313 kcals, protein 3g, carbs 65g, fat 7g, sat fat 4g, fibre 5g, sugar 65g, salt 0.06g*

# Vanilla-yogurt ice with honeyed pink grapefruit

. . . . . . . . . . . . . . . . . . . . . .

This luscious dessert is low in fat, but you'd never know it.

🕐 30 minutes, plus 4 hours or overnight freezing   🥧 6

- 200g/8oz golden caster sugar
- 1 vanilla pod, split and seeds scraped out
- 2 x 500g tubs natural yogurt
- mint leaves, to decorate

**FOR THE HONEYED PINK GRAPEFRUIT & SAUCE**
- 3 pink grapefruit
- 4 tbsp honey

1 Put the sugar in a bowl, then rub in the vanilla seeds. Stir in the yogurt until the sugar dissolves. Churn the mixture in an ice-cream maker, according to the manufacturer's instructions. Meanwhile, line a 1kg loaf tin with cling film. Once churned, spoon the frozen yogurt into the tin, cover and freeze for at least 4 hours or overnight. If you don't have an ice-cream maker, freeze the yogurt mixture for 4–6 hours, stirring every hour.

2 Segment the grapefruit, catching the juice in a bowl – you should get about 200ml/7fl oz. Put the juice in a pan with the honey, simmer for 10–15 minutes until thickened, gently stir in the segments, then cool.

3 Take the yogurt ice from the freezer about 10 minutes before you want to serve it. Cut into slices and serve topped with the grapefruit, honeyed sauce and mint leaves.

. . . . . . . . . . . . . . . . . . . . . . . . . .
*PER SERVING 301 kcals, protein 8g, carbs 60g, fat 5g, sat fat 3g, fibre 1g, sugar 60g, salt 0.29g*

# Blackcurrant & mint sorbet

Making your own sorbet is easier than you think, and the sharpness of these currants is fantastically refreshing after a rich curry.

🕐 35 minutes, plus 6 hours or overnight freezing   🥧 4–6

- 200g/8oz golden caster sugar
- 20g pack mint, plus some small sprigs to decorate
- 750g/1lb 10oz blackcurrants
- 4 tbsp liquid glucose
- juice 2 lemons

1 Make a syrup by stirring the sugar with 700ml/1¼ pints boiling water until dissolved, then steep the mint sprigs in it until cool, about 15 minutes. Discard the mint.

2 Cook the blackcurrants in the syrup with the glucose for about 5 minutes until the fruit is soft. Whizz in a food processor, then strain into a bowl through a metal sieve, pressing it through with the back of a spoon to remove the pips. Stir in the lemon juice and cool.

3 Churn in an ice-cream maker according to the manufacturer's instructions until it becomes a thick slush, then freeze for 6 hours or overnight. Or pour into a shallow freezer container and remove 3–4 times to stir it as it freezes. Remove from the freezer about 10 minutes before serving, and decorate with the extra mint sprigs.

*PER SERVING (4) 301 kcals, protein 2g, carbs 78g, fat none, sat fat none, fibre 7g, sugar 56g, salt 0.08g*

# Coconut panna cotta with pineapple salsa

An Asian twist on a classic Italian dessert – this is a stunning pudding for a special meal.

🕐 25 minutes, plus 2–48 hours chilling   🍴 6

- 2 x 400ml cans coconut milk
- 400ml/14fl oz full-fat milk
- 100g/4oz caster sugar
- 1 vanilla pod, split and seeds scraped out
- 2 x 12g sachets powdered gelatine
- 85g/3oz caster sugar
- 25g/1oz knob ginger, thinly sliced
- handful coconut chips, toasted
- 250g pack fresh pineapple, cut into small pieces
- 1 red chilli, deseeded and finely chopped

1 Put both milks, the sugar, vanilla pod and seeds into a pan. Bring to the boil, then remove from the heat and infuse for 5 minutes before discarding the pod.

2 Whisk the gelatine with 200ml/7fl oz of the hot-milk mixture until dissolved (return to a gentle heat if necessary). Stir into the rest of the hot milk and pour into six 200ml metal dariole moulds. Chill for at least 2 hours or up to 2 days, until firm with a slight wobble.

3 Tip the sugar, ginger and 100ml/3½fl oz water into a small pan. Bring to the boil, simmer for 5–10 minutes until slightly syrupy. Cool, then discard the ginger.

4 To serve, dip each mould into hot water, then turn out on to a plate. Top with toasted coconut, some pineapple and chopped chilli, and drizzle with the ginger syrup.

*PER SERVING 418 kcals, protein 8g, carbs 44g, fat 25g, sat fat 21g, fibre 1g, sugar 44g, salt 0.49g*

# Bonny lassis

This lassi is equally good served before, during or after a meal – and can be easily doubled to serve more.

🕙 10 minutes  🥧 2  ◑ Easily doubled

- 1 mango
- 2 scoops mango sorbet
- 150g pot natural yogurt
- splash milk
- 2 tsp chopped pistachio nuts
- few mint sprigs, to decorate

1 Peel and stone the mango then roughly chop the flesh. Whizz in a blender with the mango sorbet and yogurt.
2 Thin the blended mango yogurt with milk until you have a drinkable consistency, then pour into two glasses and top with chopped pistachios and mint sprigs.

*PER SERVING 227 kcals, protein 6g, carbs 43g, fat 5g, sat fat 2g, fibre 4g, sugar 41g, salt 0.18g*

# Pineapple & banana pancakes

These little tropical pancakes will disappear quickly – pile on a platter with small bowls of honey and yogurt, and let everyone help themselves.

🕐 20 minutes   🥧 4

- 100g/4oz fresh or drained canned pineapple
- 1 banana
- 100g/4oz self-raising flour
- 1 tsp baking powder
- 1 tsp ground cinnamon
- 3 tbsp light muscovado sugar
- 1 egg
- 100ml/3½fl oz milk
- sunflower oil, for frying
- Greek yogurt and clear honey, to serve

1 Roughly chop the pineapple and slice the banana, and set aside.

2 Tip the flour, baking powder, cinnamon and sugar into a bowl and mix well. Make a well in the centre, crack in the egg, then stir the egg into the flour mix, adding the milk gradually to make a soft batter.

3 Stir the pineapple and banana into the batter. Heat a little oil in a non-stick frying pan then add the fruity batter in heaped spoonfuls, spaced well apart to allow them to spread. When bubbles appear on the surface, flip the pancakes over and cook until light golden.

4 Cook all the pancakes and keep them warm. Serve 2–3 pancakes per person with a spoonful of yogurt and a little honey drizzled over the top.

*PER SERVING 230 kcals, protein 6g, carbs 42g, fat 6g, sat fat 1g, fibre 1g, sugar 11g, salt 0.7g*

# Mango with sticky rice

· · · · · · · · · · · · · · · · · · · ·

If you don't have a microwave, put the rice in a pan with the coconut, sugar and 200ml/7fl oz water. Simmer for 30 minutes and stir until all the liquid is absorbed.

🕐 45 minutes, plus 2 hours chilling   🥧 4

- 175g/6oz Thai fragrant rice
- 250ml carton coconut cream
- 85g/3oz caster sugar
- 1 ripe mango, sliced, to serve

**FOR THE MANGO SAUCE**

- 1 large ripe mango, peeled and flesh cut into chunks
- 1 tsp lime juice
- 2 tbsp caster sugar, or to taste

1 Put the rice in a microwaveable dish and stir in the coconut cream, caster sugar and 200ml/7fl oz water. Cover with cling film, pierce and microwave on Medium for 5 minutes.

2 Stir the rice then microwave on Defrost for a further 20–25 minutes until the liquid has been absorbed and the rice is tender and sticky.

3 Spoon the rice into an 18cm-square tin and spread out evenly in a layer. Cover and chill for about 2 hours.

4 Make the sauce by whizzing the mango chunks with the lime juice, and as much sugar as you wish, in a food processor until smooth.

5 Once the rice is firm, cut into 12–16 pieces. Serve with the sauce and a couple of mango slices.

· · · · · · · · · · · · · · · · · · · ·

*PER SERVING 527 kcals, protein 7g, carbs 80g, fat 22g, sat fat 19g, fibre 3g, sugar 46g, salt 0.02g*

# Coconut & chocolate bananas

The perfect prepare-ahead pud – leaving these to chill for a while before eating allows the flavours to merge.

🕐 20 minutes, plus 1 hour chilling     🥧 4

- 4 bananas
- 50g/2oz milk chocolate
- 50g/2oz caster sugar
- ½ x 400ml can coconut milk
- 200ml tub crème fraîche

1 Peel the bananas and thickly slice. Roughly chop the chocolate and set aside.
2 In a frying pan, toss the bananas with half the sugar, then fry for a few minutes until the bananas are slightly caramelized and the sugar has melted. Divide the bananas among four large ramekin dishes or glasses.
3 Whisk the remaining sugar with the coconut milk and crème fraîche, then divide among the four dishes. Sprinkle over the chopped chocolate and chill for 1 hour before serving.

*PER SERVING 478 kcals, protein 4g, carbs 46g, fat 32g, sat fat 22g, fibre 1g, sugar 44g, salt 0.2g*

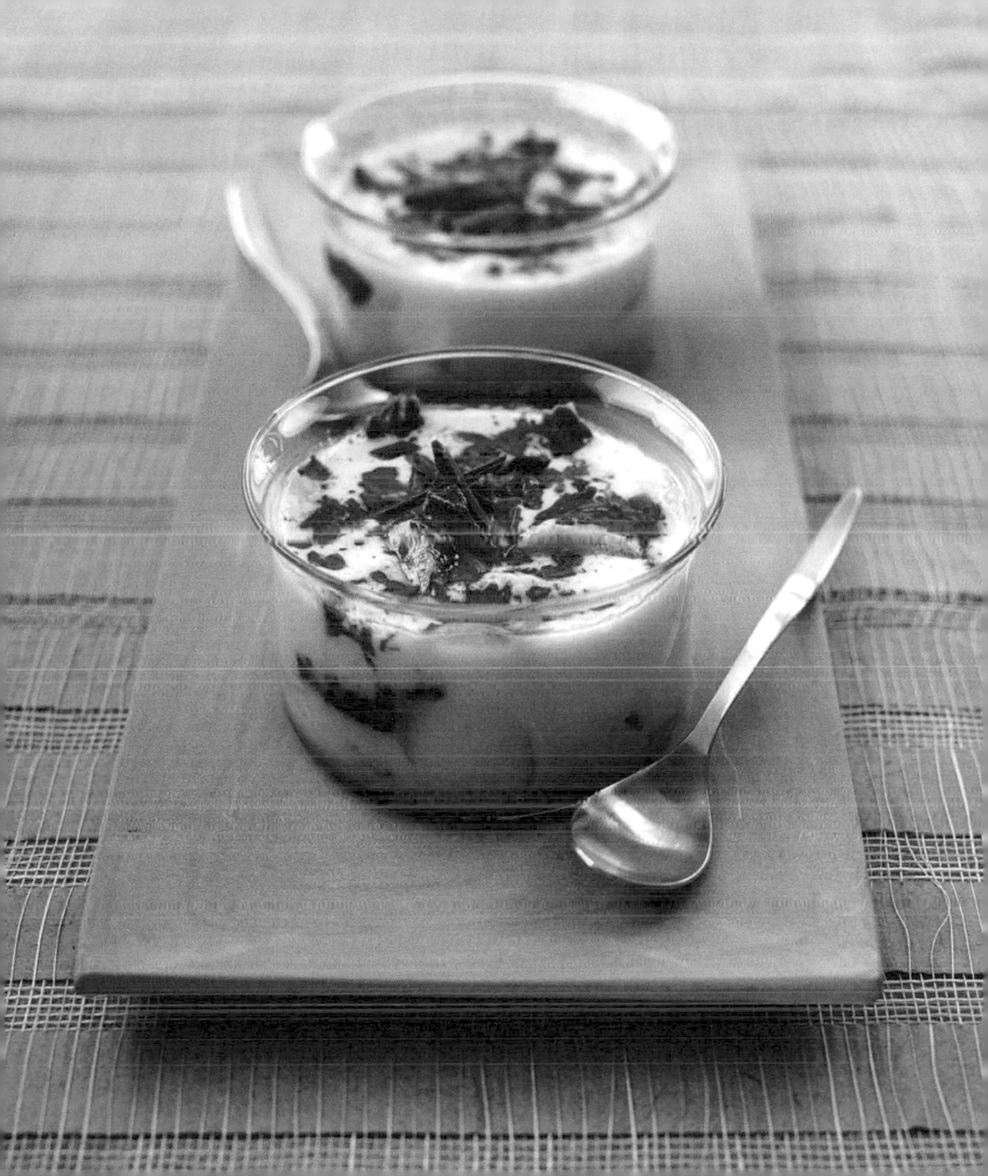

# Creamy saffron yogurt

This creamy dessert is called shrikhand and is very popular along the west coast of India.

🕐 40 minutes    🍰 6

- 700g/1lb 9oz Greek yogurt
- 2 tsp green cardamom pods
- 100g/4oz golden caster sugar
- 8–10 saffron threads
- 1 tsp milk
- 1 tbsp shelled pistachio nuts, slivered, to decorate
- 1 large ripe mango, sliced, to serve

1 Put a piece of muslin or thick kitchen paper in a large sieve set over a large bowl. Spoon the yogurt into the sieve, cover with another piece of muslin or 2 sheets kitchen paper and set aside at room temperature for 25–30 minutes (this is done to remove excess moisture).

2 Remove the seeds from the cardamom pods and crush them using a pestle and mortar – you will need 1 teaspoon ground cardamom.

3 Discard the kitchen paper or muslin, scrape the yogurt into a bowl and stir in the sugar. Mix the saffron threads with the milk, then add both to the yogurt with the ground cardamom, and mix well. Divide among six small glasses, scatter with pistachio slivers and serve with fresh mango slices.

# Spiced Indian tea

A deliciously sweet, gently spiced tea that is excellent at the end of a meal to aid digestion. Use a strong, full-bodied blend of tea such as Assam.

🕐 4 minutes   🥧 6

- 400ml/14fl oz full-fat milk
- ½ x finger-length knob ginger, bruised
- 5 cardamom pods, lightly crushed
- 5 rounded tsp loose Indian tea
- 3 tbsp caster sugar

1 Tip the milk into a large pan with 700ml/ 1¼ pints water. Add the ginger and cardamom pods, and bring to the boil. Stir in the tea, then simmer for 2–3 minutes only.
2 Strain, then stir in the sugar before serving in small cups.

*PER SERVING 77 kcals, protein 2g, carbs 11g, fat 3g, sat fat 2g, fibre none, sugar 11g, salt 0.07g*

# Index

# Also available from BBC Books and Good Food

Jill Tomlinson

# *The Owl who was Afraid of the Dark*

Plop was a baby Barn Owl, and he lived with his Mummy and Daddy at the top of a very tall tree in a field.

Plop was fat and fluffy.

He had a beautiful heart-shaped ruff.

He had enormous, round eyes.

He had very knackety knees.

In fact he was exactly the same as every baby Barn Owl that has ever been – except for one thing.

Plop was afraid of the dark.

*Also by Jill Tomlinson*

The Aardvark Who Wasn't Sure
The Cat Who Wanted To Go Home
The Gorilla Who Wanted To Grow Up
The Hen Who Wouldn't Give Up
The Otter Who Wanted To Know
Penguin's Progress

Jill Tomlinson

# The Owl who was Afraid of the Dark

*Illustrated by Susan Hellard*

Mammoth

*for Philip*
*and, of course, D.H.*

First published in Great Britain 1968
by Methuen & Co Limited
This new edition published 1992 by Mammoth
an imprint of Egmont Children's Books Ltd
239 Kensington High Street, London W8 6SA

Reprinted 1992 (four times), 1993 (five times), 1994 (five times),
1995 (four times), 1996 (four times), 1997 (three times),
1998 (three times), 1999 (twice)

Text copyright © 1968 The Estate of Jill Tomlinson
Illustrations copyright © 1991 Susan Hellard

ISBN 0 7497 0795 X

A CIP catalogue record for this title
is available from the British Library

Printed and bound in Great Britain
by Cox & Wyman Ltd, Reading, Berkshire

# CONTENTS

## DARK IS EXCITING

Plop was a baby Barn Owl, and he lived with his Mummy and Daddy at the top of a very tall tree in a field.

Plop was fat and fluffy.

He had a beautiful heart-shaped ruff.

He had enormous, round eyes.

He had very knackety knees.

In fact he was exactly the same as every baby Barn Owl that has ever been – except for one thing.

Plop was afraid of the dark.

"You *can't* be afraid of the dark,"

6

said his Mummy. "Owls are *never* afraid of the dark."

"This one is," Plop said.

"But owls are *night* birds," she said.

Plop looked down at his toes. "I don't want to be a night bird," he mumbled. "I want to be a day bird."

"You *are* what you *are*," said Mrs Barn Owl firmly.

"Yes, I know," agreed Plop, "and what I are is afraid of the dark."

"Oh dear," said Mrs Barn Owl. It was clear that she was going to need a lot of patience. She shut her eyes and tried to think how best she could help Plop not to be afraid. Plop waited.

His mother opened her eyes again. "Plop, you are only afraid of the dark because you don't know about it. What *do* you know about the dark?"

"It's black," said Plop.

7

"Well, that's wrong for a start. It can be silver or blue or grey or lots of other colours, but almost never black. What else do you know about it?"

"I don't like it," said Plop. "I do not like it AT ALL."

"That's not *knowing* something," said his mother. "That's *feeling* something. I don't think you know anything about the dark at all."

"Dark is nasty," Plop said loudly.

"You don't know that. You have never had your beak outside the nest-hole after dusk. I think you had better go down into the world and find out a lot more about the dark before you make up your mind about it."

"Now?" said Plop.

"Now," said his mother.

Plop climbed out of the nest-hole and wobbled along the branch outside. He

8

peeped over the edge. The world seemed to be a very long way down.

"I'm not a very good lander," he said. "I might spill myself."

"Your landing will improve with practice," said his mother. "Look! There's a little boy down there on the edge of the wood collecting sticks. Go and talk to him about it."

"Now?" said Plop.

"Now," said his mother. So Plop shut his eyes, took a deep breath, and fell off his branch.

His small white wings carried him down, but, as he said, he was not a good lander. He did seven very fast somersaults past the little boy.

"Ooh!" cried the little boy. "A giant Catherine-wheel!"

"Actually," said the Catherine-wheel, picking himself up, "I'm a Barn Owl."

"Oh yes – so you are," said the little boy with obvious disappointment. "Of course, you couldn't be a firework yet. Dad says we can't have the fireworks until it gets dark. Oh, I wish it would hurry up and get dark *soon*."

"You *want* it to get dark?" said Plop in amazement.

"Oh, YES," said the little boy. "DARK IS EXCITING. And tonight is specially exciting because we're going to have fireworks."

"What are fireworks?" asked Plop. "I don't think owls have them – not Barn Owls, anyway."

"Don't you?" said the little boy. "Oh, you poor thing. Well, there are rockets, and flying saucers, and volcanoes, and

10

golden rain, and sparklers, and . . ."

"But what *are* they?" begged Plop. "Do you eat them?"

"NO!" laughed the little boy. "Daddy sets fire to their tails and they *whoosh* into the air and fill the sky with coloured stars – well, the rockets, that is. I'm allowed to hold the sparklers."

"What about the volcanoes? And the golden rain? What do they do?"

"Oh, they sort of burst into showers of stars. The golden rain *pours* – well, like rain."

"And the flying saucers?"

"Oh, they're super! They whizz round your head and make a sort of *wheeee* noise. I like them best."

"I think I would like fireworks," said Plop.

"I'm sure you would," the little boy said. "Look here, where do you live?"

11

"Up in that tree – in the top flat. There are squirrels farther down."

"That big tree in the middle of the field? Well, you can watch our fireworks from there! That's our garden – the one with the swing. You look out as soon as it gets dark . . ."

"Does it *have* to be dark?" asked Plop.

"Of course it does! You can't see fireworks unless it's dark. Well, I must go. These sticks are for the bonfire."

"Bonfire?" said Plop. "What's that?"

"You'll see if you look out tonight. Goodbye!"

"Goodbye," said Plop, bobbing up and down in a funny little bow.

He watched the boy run across the field, and then took a little run himself, spread his wings, and fluttered up to the landing branch. He slithered along

it on his tummy and dived head first into the nest-hole.

"Well?" said his mother.

"The little boy says DARK IS EXCITING."

"And what do you think, Plop?"

"I still do not like it AT ALL," said Plop, "but I'm going to watch the fireworks – if you will sit by me."

"I will sit by you," said his mother.

"So will I," said his father, who had just woken up. "I like fireworks."

So that is what they did.

When it began to get dark, Plop waddled to the mouth of the nest-hole and peered out cautiously.

"Come on, Plop! I think they're starting," called Mr Barn Owl. He was already in position on a big branch at the very top of the tree. "We shall see beautifully from here."

Plop took two brave little steps out of the nest-hole.

"I'm here," said his mother quietly. "Come on."

So together, wings almost touching, they flew up to join Mr Barn Owl.

14

They were only just in time. There were flames leaping and crackling at the end of the little boy's garden. "That must be the bonfire!" squeaked Plop.

Hardly had Plop got his wings tucked away, when "*WHOOSH!*" – up went a rocket and spat out a shower of green stars. "Ooooh!" said Plop, his eyes like saucers.

A fountain of dancing stars sprang up from the ground – and another and another. "Ooooh!" said Plop again.

"You sound like a Tawny owl," said his father. "Goodness! What's that?"

Something was whizzing about leaving bright trails of squiggles behind it and making a loud "Wheeee!" noise.

"Oh, that's a flying saucer," said Plop.

"Really?" his father said. "I've never

15

seen one of those before. You seem to know all about it. What's that fizzy one that keeps jigging up and down?"

"I expect that's my friend with a sparkler. Oooooh! There's a me!"

"I beg your pardon?" said Plop's father.

"It's a Catherine-wheel! The little boy thought I was a Catherine-wheel when I landed. Oh, isn't it beautiful? And he thought *I* was one!"

Mr Barn Owl watched the whirling, sparking circles spinning round and round.

"That must have been quite a landing!" he said.

## DARK IS KIND

When the very last firework had faded away, Mr Barn Owl turned to Plop.

"Well, son," he said. "I'm off hunting now. Would you like to come?"

Plop looked at the darkness all around them. It seemed even blacker after the bright fireworks. "Er – not this time, thank you, Daddy. I can't see; I've got stars in my eyes."

"I see," said his father. "In that case I shall have to go by myself." He floated off into the darkness like a great white moth.

Plop turned in distress to his mother.

"I *wanted* to go with him. I *want* to like the dark. It's just that I don't seem to be able to."

"You will be able to, Plop. I'm quite sure about that."

"I'm not sure," said Plop.

"Well, I *am*," his mother said. "Now, come on. You'd better have your rest. You were awake half the day."

So Plop had his midnight rest, and when he woke up, his father was back with his dinner. Plop swallowed it in one huge gulp. "That was nice," he said. "What was it?"

"A mouse," said Mr Barn Owl.

"I like mouse," said Plop. "What's next?"

"I have no idea," his father said. "It's Mummy's turn now. You'll have to wait till she gets back."

18

Plop was always hungry, and his mother and father were kept very busy bringing him food all night long. When daylight came, they were very tired and just wanted to go to sleep.

"Bedtime, Plop," said Mrs Barn Owl.

"I don't want to go to bed," said Plop. "I want to be a day bird."

"Well, *I* am a night bird," said his mother. "And if your father and I don't get any sleep today, *you* won't get anything to eat tonight."

Plop did not like the sound of that at all, so he drew himself up straight and tall – well, as tall as he could – and tried to go to sleep.

He did sleep for half the morning, but then he woke up full of beans – or perhaps it was mouse – and he just could not go back to sleep again.

He jiggled up and down on the

19

branch where his poor parents were trying to roost. He practised standing on one leg, and taking off, and landing, and other important things that a little owl has to learn to do. Then he thought he would try out his voice. He tried to make a real, grown-up Barn Owl noise.

"EEeek!" he screeched. "EEEEEK!"

It sounded like the noise a cat makes if you accidentally tread upon its tail. Plop was very pleased with it.

Mrs Barn Owl was not. She half opened one bleary eye. "Plop, dear," she said. "Wouldn't you like to go down into the world again and find out some more about the dark?"

"Now?" said Plop.

"Now," said his mother.

"Don't you want to hear my screech first? It's getting jolly good."

"I heard it," Mrs Barn Owl said

"Look, there's an old lady in a deck-chair down there in that garden. Go and disturb – I mean, go and find out what she thinks about the dark."

So Plop shut his eyes, took a deep breath, and fell off his branch.

He did not get his wings working in time. He fell faster and faster and

21

finally plunged at the old lady's feet with an earth-shaking thump.

"Gracious!" cried the old lady. "A thunderbolt!"

"A-a-a-actually, I'm a Barn Owl," said the thunderbolt when he had got his breath back.

"Really?" said the old lady, peering at Plop over the top of her glasses. "I do beg your pardon. My eyes are not as good as they used to be. How nice of you to – er – drop in."

"Well, it wasn't nice of me, exactly," Plop said truthfully. "I came to ask you about something."

"Did you?" said the old lady. "Now what could that be, I wonder?"

"I wanted to ask you about the dark. You see, I'm a bit afraid of it, and that's rather awkward for an owl. We're supposed to be night birds."

22

"That is a problem," said the old lady. "Have you tried carrots?"

"What?"

"Don't say 'what', say 'I beg your pardon' if you don't hear the first time. I said, have you tried carrots? Wonderful things, carrots."

"I don't think owls have carrots – not Barn Owls, anyway."

"Oh. A pity. I've always sworn by carrots for helping one to see in the dark."

"I *can* see in the dark," said Plop. "I can see for miles and miles."

"Now, don't boast. It is not nice for little boys to boast." The old lady leaned forward and peered closely at Plop. "I suppose you are a little boy? It's so difficult to tell, these days. They all look the same."

"Yes," said Plop. "I'm a boy owl, and

23

I want to go hunting with Daddy, but he always goes hunting in the dark, and I'm afraid of it."

"How very odd," said the old lady. "Now, I love the dark. I expect you will when you are my age. DARK IS KIND."

"Tell me," Plop said.

"*Please*," said the old lady. "Such a little word, but it works wonders."

"Tell me, please," said Plop obediently.

"Well, now," the old lady began. "Dark is kind in all sorts of ways. Dark hides things – like shabby furniture and the hole in the carpet. It hides my wrinkles and my gnarled old hands. I can forget that I'm old in the dark."

"I don't think owls get wrinkles," said Plop. "Not Barn Owls, anyway. They just get a bit moth-eaten looking."

24

"Don't interrupt!" said the old lady. "It is very rude to interrupt. Where was I? Yes – dark is kind when you are old. I can sit in the dark and *remember*. I remember my dear husband, and my children when they were small, and all the good times we had together. I am never lonely in the dark."

"I haven't much to remember, yet," said Plop. "I'm rather new, you see."

"Dark is quiet, too," said the old lady, looking hard at Plop. "Dark is restful – unlike a little owl I know."

"Me?" said Plop.

"You," said the old lady. "When I was a little girl, children were seen but not heard."

"I'm not children," said Plop. "I'm a Barn Owl."

"Same thing," said the old lady. "You remind me very much of my son

William when he was about four. He had the same knackety knees."

"Are my knees knackety?" asked Plop, squinting downwards. "I can't see them. My tummy gets in the way."

"Very," said the old lady, "but I expect they'll straighten out in time. William's did. Now, I'm going indoors to have a little rest."

Plop was surprised. "I thought it was only owls who slept in the daytime," he said. "Are you a night bird, too?"

The old lady smiled. "No, just an old bird. A very tired old bird."

"Goodbye, then. I'll go now," said Plop. "Thank you for telling me about the dark."

He fluttered up to the old lady's shoulder and nibbled her ear very gently.

The old lady was enchanted. "An

owl kiss!" she said. "How very kind."

Plop jumped down again and bobbed his funny little bow.

"Such charming manners!" said the old lady.

Then Plop took a little run, spread

his wings, and flew up to the landing branch.

"Well?" said his mother.

"The old lady says DARK IS KIND."

"And what do you think, Plop?"

"I still do not like it AT ALL. Do you think my knees are knackety?"

"Of course," said his mother. "All little Barn Owls have knackety knees."

"Oh, good," said Plop. "And what do you think the old lady said? She said children should be seen but not heard!"

Mr Barn Owl opened one sleepy eye: "Hear! Hear!" he said.

## DARK IS FUN

That evening when it was getting dark,
Mr Barn Owl invited Plop to go hunting with him again. "Coming, son?" he
said. "It's a lovely night."

"Er – not this time, thank you,
Daddy," said Plop, who was sitting
just outside the nest-hole. "I'm busy."

"You don't look busy," Mr Barn Owl
said. "What are you doing?"

"I am busy *remembering*," said Plop.

"I see," said his father. "In that case

29

I shall have to go by myself." He swooped off into the darkness like a great, silent jet aeroplane.

"What are you remembering, Plop?" asked his mother.

"I'm remembering what the old lady said about dark being kind. She says she is never lonely in the dark because she has so much to remember."

"Well then," said Mrs Barn Owl, "this would seem to be a good moment for me to slip out and do a little hunting."

"You're not going to leave me by myself!" said Plop.

"I shan't be very long. I'll try to bring you back something nice."

"But I shall be lonely."

"No, you won't. You just keep busy remembering like the old lady said."

Plop watched his mother float off into the darkness like a white feather.

The darkness seemed to come towards him and wrap itself around him.

"Dark is kind," Plop muttered to himself. "Dark is kind. Oh dear, what shall I remember?" He closed his eyes and tried to remember something to remember. Fireworks! He would remember the fireworks. He had enjoyed them. The darkness had been spotted and striped and sploshed with coloured lights above the glow of the bonfire. He still had stars in his eyes when he thought of it.

Shouts – happy shouts – from under his tree brought Plop back from his remembering. He opened his eyes and peered down through the leaves. There were people running about in his field, and flames were flickering from a pile of sticks. Another bonfire! Did that mean more fireworks?

Plop watched excitedly. He could see now that the people running about were boys – quite big boys in shorts. They were collecting more wood for the fire.

Suddenly they all disappeared into the woods with squeals and yells. All but one, that is. There was one boy left, sitting on a log near the fire.

Plop forgot about being afraid of the dark. He had to know what was going on. So he shut his eyes, took a deep breath, and fell off his branch.

The ground was nearer than he expected it to be, and he landed with an enormous thud.

"Coo!" said the boy on the log. "A roly-poly pudding! Who threw that?"

"Nobody threw me – I just came," said the roly-poly pudding, "and actually I'm a Barn Owl."

"So you are," said the boy. "Have you fallen out of your nest?"

Plop drew himself up as tall as he could. "I did not fall – I flew," he said. "I'm just not a very good lander, that's all. I came to see if you were going to have fireworks, as a matter of fact."

"Fireworks?" said the boy. "No. What made you think that?"

"Well, the bonfire," Plop said.

"Bonfire!" said the boy. "This is no

*bonfire!* This is a camp-fire – and I'm guarding it till the others get back."

"Where have they gone?" asked Plop.

"They've gone to play games in the dark, lucky things."

"Do you *like* playing games in the dark?" asked Plop.

"It's super!" said the boy. "DARK IS FUN. Even quite ordinary games like Hide-and-Seek are fun in the dark. My favourite is the game where one of you stands outside a 'home' with a torch in his hand, and shines it on anything he sees or hears moving. The rest of you have to creep past him and 'home' without being spotted. It's super!"

There was a crash, and a yell of "Scumbo! Got you!" from the wood.

"There – they're playing it now. Old Scumbo always gets caught first. He's got such big feet. You have to creep

34

like a shadow not to be caught. Oh, it *would* be my turn to guard the fire."

"What's the fire for?" asked Plop.

"Well, we cook potatoes in it, and make cocoa, and sing round it."

"What for?"

"What for? Because it's fun, that's why, and because Boy Scouts have always had camp-fires."

"Is that what you are? A Boy Scout?"

"Of course, silly, or I wouldn't be here, would I? I must put some more wood on the fire."

Plop watched the Boy Scout build up the fire. "Could – could I be a Boy Scout, do you think?" he asked.

"I doubt it," said the Scout. "You're a bit on the small side. I suppose you could be a Cub, but you have to be eight years old."

"I'm eight weeks," said Plop.

"Looks as if you'll have a long wait, then, doesn't it?" said the Scout. "Anyway," – he grinned – "you'd look jolly silly in the uniform!"

Plop looked so disappointed that the Scout added, "Never mind. You can stay for the sing-song tonight."

"Oh, can I!" cried Plop. "That would be soo – super!"

"You'd better go home and ask your mother first, though."

So Plop flew up to the nest-hole – and found his mother waiting.

"Where have you been?" she said. She sounded a bit cross, like all mothers when they have been worried.

"I've been talking to a Boy Scout, and he says DARK IS FUN, and he says I can stay for the camp-fire, so can I, Mummy, please?"

"Well, yes, all right," she said.

"Oh, super!" said Plop.

So Plop was a Boy Scout for a night.
He sat on his new friend's shoulder
and was introduced to all the others.
They made a great fuss of him and he

had a wonderful time. He did not care for cocoa, but he enjoyed a small potato. His friend blew on it for him to cool it, because he knew that owls swallow their food whole, and a hot potato in the tummy would have been very uncomfortable for Plop!

The Scouts huddled round the fire and sang and sang while the sparks danced. They sang funny songs and sad songs, long songs and short songs. Plop did not sing because he wanted to listen, but every now and then he got a bit excited and fluttered round the boys' heads crying "Eeek! Eeeek!" and everybody laughed.

They sang until the fire had sunk to a deep, red glow and Plop had turned quite pink in its light.

Then it was time to go home, for the boys and for Plop. And when Plop had

said goodbye to them all, and bowed
and bowed till he ached, he spread his
wings and flew up to the landing
branch.

"Well?" said his mother.

"I told you. The Boy Scout says
DARK IS FUN."

"And what do you think, Plop?"

"I still do not like it AT ALL – but I
think camp-fires are super! Did you
bring me something special?"

"I did."

Plop swallowed it in one gulp.

"That was nice," he said.

"What was it?"

"A grasshopper."

"I like grass-
hopper," said Plop.
"What's next?"

## DARK IS NECESSARY

Plop asked "What's next" a great
many times during that night. He sat
just outside the nest-hole making loud
snoring noises. He was not asleep –
just hungry. Owls always snore when
they're hungry.

"Oh, Plop. I shall be glad when you
can hunt for yourself," said Mrs Barn
Owl wearily when Plop had gulped
down his seventh – or was it his
eighth? – dinner.

"What's next?" asked Plop.

"Nothing," said his mother. "You

can't possibly have room for anything else."

"I have," said Plop. "My mouse place is full up, but my grasshopper place isn't."

"That's just too bad," said Mrs Barn Owl, stretching and settling herself down to roost.

Mr Barn Owl swooped in, clapping his wings. He dropped something at Plop's feet. Plop swallowed it in one gulp. It was deliciously slippery.

"That was nice," he said. "What was it?"

"A fish," said his father.

"I like fish," said Plop. "What's next?"

"Bed," said Mr Barn Owl. He kissed his wife good night – or good day, I suppose it was – and settled himself to roost.

Plop made a few hopeful snoring noises, but it was clear that the feast was over. He wobbled into the nest-hole and was soon fast asleep himself.

It was well into the afternoon when he woke up. He came out on to the landing branch and looked around. His parents were still drawn up as still as carvings, but the squirrels from downstairs were chasing each other up and down the trunk, their tails flying behind them. Plop watched them for a bit. One of them scuttled along the branch just below Plop's and then stopped abruptly and began to wash his face. He did not know that Plop was there – after all, owls are *supposed* to be asleep during the daytime.

Plop could not resist it. He bent down through the leaves and let out his very loudest "Eeeek!"

The squirrel jumped into the air like a jack-in-a-box, his ears a-quiver and his eyes like marbles. He flashed down the trunk and vanished into his hole.

Plop jumped up and down with delight. But of course he had done it again: he had woken his mother.

"Plop!"

"Yes, Mummy?"

"Go and find out some more about the dark, please, dear."

"Now?" said Plop.

"Now," said his mother. "Go and ask that little girl what she thinks about it."

"What little girl?"

"That little girl sitting down there – the one with the pony-tail."

"Little girls don't have *tails*."

"This one does. Go on now or you'll miss her."

So Plop shut his eyes, took a deep breath, and fell off his branch.

His landing was a little better than usual. He bounced three times and rolled gently towards the little girl's feet.

"Oh! A woolly ball!" cried the little girl.

"Actually I'm a Barn Owl," said the woolly ball.

"An owl? Are you sure?" she said, putting out a grubby finger and prodding Plop's round fluffy tummy.

"Quite sure," said Plop, backing away and drawing himself up tall.

"Well, there's no need to be huffy," said the little girl. "You bounced. You must expect to be mistaken for a ball if you will go bouncing about the place. I've never met an owl before. Do you say Tu-whit-a-woo?"

"No," said Plop. "That's Tawny Owls."

"Oh, you can't be a proper owl, then," said the little girl. "*Proper* owls say 'Tu-whit-a-woo' !"

"I *am* a proper owl!" said Plop,

getting very cross.
"I am a Barn Owl,
and Barn Owls go
*Eeeek* like that."

"Oh, don't *do*
that!" said the little
girl, putting her
hands over her ears.

"Well, you shouldn't have made me
cross," said Plop. "Anyway – *you* can't
be a proper girl."

"*What* did you say?" said the little
girl, taking her hands off her ears.

"I said you're not a proper girl. Girls
don't have *tails*. Squirrels have tails,
rabbits have tails, mice . . ."

"This is a *pony* tail," said the little
girl. "It's the longest one in the class,"
she added proudly.

"But why do you want to look like a
pony?" asked Plop.

"Because – oh, because it's the fashion," said the little girl. "Don't you know *anything*?"

"Not much," agreed Plop. "Mummy says that that is why I'm afraid of the dark – because I don't know anything about it. Do *you* like the dark?"

The little girl looked at Plop in surprise. "Well, of course I do," she said. "There has to be dark. DARK IS NECESSARY."

"Dark is nessessess – is whatter?"

"Necessary. We need it. We can't do without it."

"I could do without it," said Plop. "I could do without it very nicely."

"Father Christmas wouldn't come," said the little girl. "You'll have an empty stocking on Christmas day."

47

"I don't wear stockings," said Plop, "and who is Father Christmas?"

"Well, Father Christmas is a fat, jolly old man with a white beard, and he wears a red suit with a matching hat, and black boots."

"Is that the fashion?" asked Plop.

"No," said the little girl. "It's just what he always wears in pictures of him – although I don't know how anybody knows because nobody has ever seen him."

"What?" said Plop.

"Well, that's what I'm trying to tell you. *Father Christmas only comes in the dark*. He comes in the middle of the night, riding through the sky on a sledge pulled by reindeer."

"Deer?" asked Plop. "In the sky?"

"Magic deer," said the little girl. "Everything about Father Christmas is magic. Otherwise he couldn't possibly get round to all the children in the world in one night – or have enough toys for them all in his sack."

"You didn't tell me about his sack."

"He has a sack full of toys and he puts them in the children's stockings."

"In their stockings?" said Plop. "With their feet in them? There can't be much room – "

"No, silly. We hang empty stockings at the ends of our beds for him to fill. I usually borrow one of Mummy's, but last year I hung up my tights."

"And did he fill them?" breathed Plop.

"No – only one leg, but he did put a sugar mouse in the other one."

"I'd rather have had a real mouse," said Plop.

"So would I, really," said the little

girl. "I wanted a white mouse, but Mummy says that if a mouse comes into the house she will leave it, and I suppose Father Christmas didn't want me to be an orphan."

Plop was thinking. "I don't think owls have Father Christmas – not Barn Owls, anyway – and I haven't got a stocking to hang up."

"Aah, what a shame," said the little girl. "Everybody should have Father Christmas. It's so exciting waking up in the morning and feeling all the bumps in your stocking and trying to guess what is in it."

"Oh, stop it," wailed Plop. "I wish he would come to me."

"Shut your eyes," the little girl said. "Go on. Shut them and you may get a surprise."

Plop shut his eyes tight and waited.

The little girl quickly pulled off her wellington and took off a sock. She was wearing two pairs because the boots were a bit big for her.

"Open your eyes!" she said to Plop,

holding up the sock while she stood on one leg and wriggled her foot back into her wellington.

Plop opened his eyes – and then shut them again because he couldn't believe what he saw.

"Don't you want it?" said the little girl. "I know it's a bit holey, but I don't expect Father Christmas will mind."

"Oh, thank you," said Plop, taking it with his beak and then holding it in his foot. "Thank you *very* much. I'll go and hang it up at once."

"Not yet," laughed the little girl. "You'll have to wait until Christmas Eve. Well, I must go now. It must be nearly tea-time. Goodbye. I do hope Father Christmas will come to you."

"Goodbye," said Plop, bobbing his funny little bow. "You are very kind. You are a proper girl."

"And you have a very nice 'Eeek' !" said the little girl. "I'm going to practise it to make my brothers jump. EEEK!" She ran off, and Plop could hear her 'eeeking' right across the field.

Plop picked up the sock in his beak, and flew up to the landing branch.

"Well?" said his mother.

"Jah lijjle yirl shays – "  he began with his mouth full of sock. He put it down and tried again. "The little girl says DARK IS NECESSARY, because of Father Christmas coming," he said.

"And what do you think, Plop?"

"I still do not like it AT ALL – but I'm going to hang up this sock on Christmas Eve."

And Plop took his sock and put it away very carefully in a corner of the nest-hole ready for Christmas.

## DARK IS FASCINATING

Plop, having slept nearly all day, was very lively that evening – very lively and very hungry. He kept wobbling along the branch to where his father was roosting to see if by chance he were awake and ready to go hunting.

Mr Barn Owl was drawn up tall and still. He seemed hardly to be breathing. Plop stretched up on tiptoe and tried to see into his father's face. What a strong, curved beak he had.

"Daddy, are you awake?" he said loudly. "I'm hungry."

Mr Barn Owl did not open his eyes, but the beak moved.

"Go away!" it said. "I'm asleep."

Plop went away obediently – and then realised something and went back again. "Daddy! You can't be asleep. You spoke – I heard you."

"You must have imagined it," said his father, still not opening his eyes.

"You spoke," said Plop. "You're awake, so you can go hunting." He butted his father's tummy with his head. "Come on! It's getting-up time!"

Mr Barn Owl sighed and stretched. "All right, all right, you horrible owlet. What time is it?" He looked up at the sky. "Suffering bats! It isn't even dark yet! I could have had another half hour." He glared at Plop. "Dash it, I'm going to have another half hour. I will not be bullied by an addled little

– little DAY BIRD. Go away! You may wake me when it is dark, and not before, d'you understand?" He suddenly leaned forward until his huge beak was level with Plop's own little carpet tack. Plop could see two of himself reflected in his father's eyes.

"Er – yes, Daddy," he said, backing away hurriedly.

"Good," said his father, drawing himself up to sleep again. "Good day."

Plop went back to the nest-hole to complain to his mother. A sleepy Mrs Barn Owl listened sympathetically.

"Well, dear, I should go and find out some more about the world if I were you," she said. "Look! There's a young lady down there. Why don't you go and talk to her?"

Plop peered down through the leaves. Standing a little way from the tree

was someone wearing
shiny black boots, a
bright red fur coat
with a matching hat,
and what looked like
a white beard.

"That's not a young
lady!" shrieked Plop.
"That's Father Christmas!"
And he fell off his branch
in such a hurry that he forgot either to
shut his eyes *or* to take a deep breath.

He landed quite well, considering,
but lost his balance at the last moment
and toppled forward on to his face.

A gentle hand picked him up and set
him right way up again.

"Oh, you poor darling," said a sweet
young voice. "Are you all right?"

Plop looked up quickly. That voice
didn't sound right.

It wasn't a white beard – it was long blond hair.

"You're not Father Christmas at all!" he said crossly. "And I came down *specially*."

"I'm terribly sorry," said the young lady.

"And I'm not a darling. I'm a Barn Owl."

"I tell you what," the Father Christmas Lady said. "May I draw a picture of you in my Nature Sketch Book? I haven't got a Barn Owl in it."

"Me?" said Plop. "You mean *really* me?"

"Yes, please. Perhaps you could pose on that low branch for me."

Plop fluttered up to the branch and stood stiffly to attention. The Father Christmas Lady sat on a log and began to draw.

58

"I always carry my sketch book about with me in case I see something interesting," she said.

The interesting Barn Owl drew himself up proudly like a soldier in a sentry box.

But not for long. The young lady looked up from her drawing to find that her Barn Owl had completely disappeared.

"Can I see?" said a small voice down by her boot. Plop was jiggling up and down trying to see what was on the pad.

"There's not much to see, yet," she said, "but all right – you can look."

Plop looked. "I'm not bald like that!" he said indignantly.

"I haven't had time to get you properly

dressed," said the young lady.

"And you've only given me one leg."

"I'm afraid a bald, one-legged Barn Owl is all there's going to be unless you keep still."

Plop really tried very hard after that, and he only got down three or four times to see how she was getting on.

He could hardly believe his eyes when it was finished. "Is that really me?" he said. "I look just like Daddy – well, almost."

"Yes, that's really you," she said. "I keep one end of the book for animals and birds that come out in the day-time and the other end for night creatures. I've put you with them, of course."

"Oh," said Plop. "Er – of course."

"All the most interesting ones are your end," the young lady went on. "I think DARK IS FASCINATING."

"I – er – *tell* me about it," said Plop. (Well, it was too late now to tell her that she had got him at the wrong end of the book!)

"Hop up then," said the young lady, holding out a finger and taking Plop on to her lap, "and I'll show you what good company you are in. Look – here are some badgers."

Plop looked at the big black and white animals with stripes down their noses. "Funny faces they've got."

"That's so they don't bump into each other in the dark," explained the young lady. "They can't see very well."

She turned over the page. "Ah! Now I think these are the most fascinating night creatures of all – bats."

 "You've got it the wrong way up," said Plop.

The Father Christmas lady laughed.

"No, I haven't. That's how bats like to be when they're not fluttering about – hanging upside down by their feet."

"Go on!" said Plop.

"Yes, really. And do you know, if you were a baby bat your mother would take you with her wherever she went, clinging to her fur. You'd get lots of rides."

"Oh, I'd like that," Plop said.

"Yes, but when you got too big to be carried, do you know what your mother would do? She'd hang you up before she went out!"

"Hang me up?" said Plop. "Upside down?"

"That's right. Now, let's see what else we can find." She turned a few pages. "Yes, here we are – oh!"

Plop was not with her.

He was rocking backwards and forwards on the low branch like one of those little wobbly men that you push. Every now and then he went a bit too far and had to waggle his wings to keep his balance.

"What are you doing?" asked the young lady.

"I'm trying to be a bat," said Plop, "but what I don't understand is how they begin. I can't *get* upside down."

"Perhaps it would be easier to be a hedgehog," said the young lady. "When they're frightened they roll themselves into a ball, look – here's a picture of one."

Plop hopped back on to her knee and inspected the hedgehog.

"His feathers could do with a bit of fluffing up," he said.

"Those aren't feathers – they're prickles. Very useful they are, too. A hedgehog can jump off quite a high fence without hurting himself because he makes himself into a prickly ball and just bounces."

"Very useful," said Plop. "I wish I had prickles." He jumped off her lap and tried to roll himself into a ball.

It was very difficult. "I don't seem to have enough bends," he said.

64

Suddenly he stopped rolling about and stayed still, listening. Then he rushed back to the young lady's lap and tried to bury himself in her coat.

"What's the matter?" she said.

"THERE'S A FUNNY NOISE," he said. "OVER THERE."

The young lady listened. There was a busy, rustling sound coming from the dry leaves under the big tree.

"Why, I do believe it's a hedgehog!"

she said. "Yes, here he is. Look!"

Plop peeped cautiously over the edge of her lap. A tiny pointed snout pushed its way through the leaves, and then a small round creature scuttled across the ground in front of them.

"They never bother to move about quietly," the young lady whispered, "because they know nobody would want to eat anything so prickly."

"Is he sure?" said Plop. "I'm so hungry I could eat anything!"

The hedgehog stopped dead and rolled himself into a tight little ball.

"He must have heard you," the young lady said reproachfully. "What a thing to say."

"Well, it's true," Plop said. "I'm starving."

"Oh, of course! You'll be going hunting with your parents now that it's

getting dark, won't you? I was forget-
ting you're a night bird."

The night bird looked down at his
toes.

"Well, I won't keep you," she went
on, "except – would you mind doing
something for me before you go? I
*would* like to hear you screech."

Plop didn't mind at all. He stuck out
his chest and gave her the most
enormous "EEEEEEEK!" he could possibly manage.

"Gorgeous!" said the young lady.

Plop bobbed his funny little bow.
Then he took off and circled round,
'eeking' for all he was worth. The
young lady waved, and then with one
final 'eeeek!' of farewell, Plop flew up
to the landing branch.

"Well?" said his mother.

"The Father Christmas Lady – you

were right, it was a lady – says DARK IS FASCINATING."

"And what do you think, Plop?"

"I still do not like it AT ALL. But what do you think? The lady drew a picture of me."

"Well, that's very special, isn't it? Nobody has ever put me in a picture."

"*And* she says my screech is gorgeous."

"She does, does she? I wondered what all that noise was about."

"Where's Daddy?"

"Out hunting."

"Oh, jolly good. I could eat a hedge-hog!"

"I wouldn't recommend it," said his mother.

## DARK IS WONDERFUL

"That was nice," said Plop when he had gulped down what his father had brought. "What was it?"

"A shrew," said his father.

"I like shrew," said Plop. "What's next?"

"A short pause," said Mrs Barn Owl. "Let your poor Daddy get his breath back."

"All right," said Plop, "but do hurry up, Daddy. Shrews are nice, but they're not very big, are they? This one feels very lonely all by itself at the bottom

69

of my tummy. It needs company."

"I don't believe there is a bottom to your tummy," said his father. "No matter how much I put into it, it is never full. Oh well, I suppose I had better go and hunt for something else to cast into the bottomless pit."

"That's what fathers are for," said Plop. "Wouldn't you like to go hunting, too, Mummy? It would be a nice change for you."

"Thank you very much," said Mrs Barn Owl. "What you really mean is that you won't have to wait so long between courses! But I will certainly go if you don't mind being left."

"Why don't you come with us?" said his father. "Then you wouldn't have to wait at all."

Plop looked round at the creeping darkness. "Er – no, thank you, Daddy,"

he said. "I have some more remembering to do."

"Right'o," said Mr Barn Owl.
"Ready, dear?"

Plop's parents took off together side
by side, their great white wings almost
touching. Plop sat outside the nest-
hole and watched them drift away into

the darkness until they melted into each other and then disappeared altogether. It took quite a long time, because the stars were coming out and Plop could see a long way by their light with his owl's eyes.

He remembered what his mother had said about dark never being black. It certainly was not black tonight. It was more of a misty grey, and the sky was pricked all over with tiny stars.

"Drat!" said a voice from somewhere below Plop.

Plop started and peered down through the leaves. There was a man with some sort of contraption set up in front of him, standing there scowling up at the cloud which had hidden the moon. What was he doing?

Plop shut his eyes, took a deep breath, and fell off his branch.

He shot through the air like a white
streak and landed with a soft bump.

"Heavens!" cried the man. "A shooting star!"

"Actually, I'm a Barn Owl," said the

73

shooting star. "What's that thing you've got there?"

"A telescope," said the man. "A Barn Owl, did you say? Well, well. I thought you were a meteor. How do you do?"

"How do I do what?" asked Plop.

"Oh – you know what I mean. How are you?"

"Hungry," said Plop. "I thought you said I was a shooting star, not a meteor."

"A meteor *is* a shooting star."

"Oh," said Plop. "What is the television for?"

"Telescope. For looking at things like the stars and planets."

"Ooh! Can I have a look, please?"

"Of course," said the man, "but it's not a very good night for it, I'm afraid. Too cloudy."

74

"I don't like the dark very much," said Plop.

"Really?" said the man. "How very odd. You must miss such a lot. DARK IS WONDERFUL."

"Tell me," said Plop. "Please."

"I'll do better than that – I'll show you," the man said. "Come and put your eye – no, no! *This* end!"

Plop had jumped up, scuttled along the telescope, and was now peering backwards between his feet into the wrong end.

"I can't see anything," he said.

"You surprise me," said the man. "Try this end."

Plop wobbled back along the telescope and the man supported him on his wrist so that his eye was level with the eye-piece.

"Now can you see anything?"

"Oh yes," said Plop. "It makes everything come nearer, doesn't it? I can see a bright, bright star. That must be very near."

"Yes – just fifty four million, million miles away, that's all."

"Million, million – !" gasped Plop.

"Yes, that's Sirius, the Dog Star. You're quite right – it is one of the nearest." Obviously million millions were nothing to the man with a telescope.

"Why is it called the Dog Star?" asked Plop.

"Because it belongs to Orion, the Great Hunter. Look! There he is. Can you see those three stars close together?"

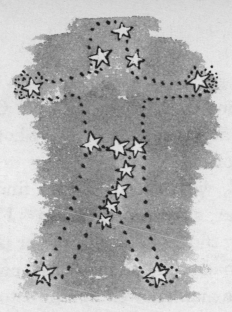

Plop drew his head back from the telescope and blinked.

"Can I change eyes?" he said. "This one's getting very tired."

"Yes, of course. Now – see if you can find the Great Hunter."

"He has three stars close together, did you say?"

"Yes – that's his belt."

"And some fainter stars behind him?"

"Yes – that's his sword."

"I've got him!" shouted Plop. "I've got Orion the Great Hunter. Oh, I never knew stars had names. Show me some more."

"Well, we'll see if we can find the Pole Star, shall we? Hang on – I have to swing the telescope round for that."

Plop had a ride on the telescope, and then the man showed him how to find the Plough and the two stars pointing straight up to the Pole Star. "That's a bright one, too, isn't it?" said Plop.

"Yes. There! Now you can find that, you need never get lost, because that star is directly over the North Pole so you'll always know where north is."

"Is that important?" asked Plop.

"Very important," said the man. "Heavens! What was that?" An eerie, long-drawn shriek had torn the peace of the night.

"Oh dear. I expect that's my Daddy," said Plop. They looked up. A ghostly, whitish form circled above them. "Yes, it is. I'd better let him know I'm here. Eeeeeek!"

"Oh!" said the man, jumping. "You should warn people when you're going to do that. You know, I've often wondered what that noise was. Now I shall know it is only you or your father."

"Or my mother," said Plop. "I really must go. Thank you very, very much for teaching me about the stars." He hopped on to the telescope and bowed his funny little bow. "Goodbye."

"Goodbye, Master Barn Owl. Good star-gazing!"

Plop flew up to join his father and together they landed on the landing branch.

"Well?" said Plop's mother.

"The man with the telescope says DARK IS WONDERFUL, and he called me 'Master Barn Owl' and . . ."

"And what do you think, Plop?"

"I know what *I* think," said Mr Barn Owl, not giving Plop a chance to reply. "I think Master Barn Owl has got a bit of a cheek to send his poor parents on an absolutely urgent search for food and then not bother to be in when they get back. I thought you were supposed to be starving?"

80

"I *am* starving," said Plop, "but did you know that the Dog Star is fifty-four million, million miles away . . ."

"Do you want your dinner or don't you?" said Mr Barn Owl.

"Oh yes," said Plop. He gobbled down what his father had brought, and he gobbled down what his mother had brought, and not only did he not ask what it was that he had just eaten, but he did not even say "What's next?"

What he said was, "Daddy, do you know how to find the Pole Star? Shall I show you?"

"By all means," said Mr Barn Owl, giving his wife a slow wink. "Anything that can take your mind off your tummy like this *must* be worth seeing!"

Plop would not rest – and so neither could Mr and Mrs Barn Owl – until he had made quite sure that they could recognise all the stars which the man with the telescope had shown him.

He was still at it at about four o'clock in the morning.

"Now are you quite sure you understand about the Pole Star?" he said to his mother, who seemed to be being a bit dense about it.

"I think so, dear," yawned Mrs Barn Owl. "You find the thing that looks like a plough but is actually a big bear – or is it a small bear? – and the Pole Star is – um – near the North Star."

"The Pole Star *is* the North Star," Plop said impatiently, "and the two stars at the front of the Plough point to it. I don't think you're really trying. You haven't been listening."

"Oh, we have," said Mr Barn Owl. "We have been listening for hours and hours. I think perhaps Mummy is just a little bit tired . . ."

"But you must know how to find the Pole Star," said Plop, "or you might get lost."

"I never get lost," said his father indignantly, "and neither does your mother. Now be a good chap and go into the nest-hole and I'll see if I can find you something nice for your supper. You can have it in bed for once, hmm?"

"Oh, all right," said Plop, "but I really do feel that you should know about these things. I'll have to try to explain again tomorrow."

Mr Barn Owl turned to his wife in horror. "Oh, no! Not tomorrow night as well! I couldn't stand it."

"Never mind, dear," said Mrs Barn Owl soothingly. "You haven't had to do nearly as much hunting as usual."

"I'm not at all sure that all this star-gazing isn't much more wearing than filling the bottomless pit!" groaned Mr Barn Owl.

"Oh, Daddy." Plop put his head out of the nest-hole. "Did I tell you about Orion? Orion is the Great Hunter and – oh, he's gone!"

"Yes, dear, he must finish his hunting before it gets light," said his mother. "Now you get back in there and mind you wash behind your ears properly. I'm coming to inspect you in a minute."

So Plop had his supper in bed. And then, like a real night owl, he slept right through the daylight hours.

## DARK IS BEAUTIFUL

When Plop woke up, it was already getting dark. He came out on to the landing branch. There was an exciting frosty nip in the air. "Now who's a day bird!" Plop shouted at the darkness. "I am what I am!"

"What *is* he bellowing about?" said Mr Barn Owl, waking up with a start.

"I believe Plop is beginning to enjoy being an owl at last," said Mrs Barn Owl, "but ssh! Pretend to be asleep."

Plop waddled up to inspect them. They were drawn up tall. Fancy sleeping on such a lovely night! Well, he wasn't going to hang about waiting for them. He might be missing something. The man with a telescope might be back, or some Boy Scouts, or anything. He was going down to see.

So Plop shut his eyes, took a deep breath, and fell off his branch.

He floated down on his little white wings and landed like a feather. Feeling very pleased with himself, he looked around.

There were two strange lamps shining from the shadows under the tree. Plop went closer, and found that the lamps were a pair of unwinking eyes, and they belonged to a big black cat. Plop waited for a minute, but what he was expecting to happen didn't.

"Aren't you going to say anything?" he said at last. "All the others did."

"What should I say?" drawled the cat.

"Well, what did you think I was?" said Plop. "I've been mistaken for a Catherine-wheel, and a thunderbolt, and a woolly ball, and a darling and a shooting star, and even a roly-poly pudding. Don't I remind you of anything?"

"You look like a baby owl to me," said the cat. Then, seeing Plop's disappointed face, he added, "but I *did* wonder for a moment whether it was starting to snow."

"You thought I was a snowflake?" said Plop, brightening.

"Yes, but then when you landed, I saw that you looked more like a fat little snowman," said the cat, "and then I knew you were a baby owl."

"Ah, but do you know what *kind* of owl I am?" said Plop.

"No," admitted the cat, "I can't say I do."

"I am a Barn Owl," Plop said.

"Really?" said the cat. "Well, I'm a House Cat, I suppose. My name is Orion."

"Orion! The Great Hunter!" breathed Plop.

"Well, thank you," said the cat, stroking his fine whiskers with a modest paw. "I am rather a good mouser, as a matter of fact, but I didn't know I was as famous as that."

"Orion," said Plop again. "Oh, I wish I had a name like that."

"What is your name?" asked the cat.

"Plop," said Plop. "Isn't it awful?"

"Oh, I don't know – it's – er – different," the cat said kindly, "and at least it's short. There's nothing short for Orion really, so I'm usually called

'Puss', which I can't say I care for."

"I shall call you Orion," said Plop.

"Thank you. Look – er – Plop. I was just going hunting. Would you like to come with me?"

"Oh," said Plop. "I don't know. I would like to, I think, but I'm not very happy about the dark."

"Oh dear. We'll have to do something about that," said Orion.

"What?" said Plop. "What can you do when you're afraid of the dark?"

"I don't believe you are afraid of the dark, really," said Orion. "You just think you are. DARK IS BEAUTIFUL. Take a night like this. Look around you. Isn't it beautiful?"

Plop looked. The moon had risen. Everything was bathed in its white light.

"I love moonlight," said the cat.

"Moonlight is magic. It turns everything it touches to silver, especially on frosty nights like this. Oh, come with me, Plop, and I will show you a beautiful world of sparkling silver – the secret night-time world of cats and owls. The daytime people are asleep. It is all ours, Plop. Will you come?"

"Yes!" said Plop. "I will. Just wait while I tell Mummy where I'm going," He flew like an arrow up to the landing branch.

"Well?" said his mother.

"Orion says that DARK IS BEAUTIFUL, and he has asked me to go hunting with him. I can go, can't I, Mummy?"

"Of course, dear. But who is Orion?"

"The Great Hunter!" said Plop. "See you later."

When Mr Barn Owl came in from his

first expedition, he found his wife a bit agitated.

"I think all that star-gazing has gone to Plop's head," she said. "He said he was going hunting with Orion the Great Hunter. That was one of the stars he showed us last night, wasn't it?"

"Well, I saw him just now with a perfectly ordinary black cat," said Mr Barn Owl. "They were pussy-footing it up among the chimney pots on those houses near the church."

"So far from home – are you *sure* it was Plop you saw?" said Mrs Barn Owl.

It was indeed Plop he had seen. Orion had taken him up to his roof-top world, the cat leading the way, climbing and leaping, Plop fluttering behind.

They sat together on the highest roof and looked down over the sleeping town, a black velvet cat and a little white powder puff of owl.

"Well?" said the cat.

"It is – it is – oh, I haven't the words for it," breathed Plop. "But you are right, Orion. I am a night bird after all. Fancy sleeping all night and missing this!"

"And this is only one sort of night,"

said Orion. "There are lots of other kinds, all beautiful. There are hot, scented summer nights; and cold windy nights when the scuffling clouds make ragged shadows across the ground; and breathless, thundery nights which are suddenly slashed with jagged white lightning; and fresh spring nights, when even the day-birds

can't bear to sleep; and muffled winter nights when snow blankets the ground and ices the houses and trees. Oh, the nights I have seen – and you will see, Plop, as a night bird."

"Yes," said Plop. "This is my world, Orion. I must go home."

"What, already? We haven't done any hunting yet, and I have lots more to show you – a glass lake with the moon floating in it, and . . ."

"I must go, Orion. I want to surprise them. Thank you for – for showing me that I'm a night bird."

He bobbed his funny little bow and the black cat solemnly bowed back. "Goodbye, Plop," he said, "and many, many Good Nights!"

Plop took off, circled once, gave a final "Eek!" of farewell, and then flew, straight and sure, back to his tree.

"Well?" said his mother.

Plop took a deep breath. "The small boy said DARK IS EXCITING. The old lady said DARK IS KIND. The Boy Scout said DARK IS FUN. The little girl said DARK IS NECESSARY. The Father Christmas Lady said DARK IS FASCINATING. The man with the telescope said DARK IS WONDERFUL and Orion the black cat says DARK IS BEAUTIFUL."

"And what do you think, Plop?"

Plop looked up at his mother with twinkling eyes. "I think," he said. "I think – DARK IS SUPER! But Sssh! Daddy's coming. Don't say anything."

Mr Barn Owl came in with a great flapping of wings. He dropped something at Plop's feet.

Plop swallowed it in one gulp. "That was nice," he said. "What was it?"

"A vole."

95

"I like vole," said Plop. "What's next?"

"Why don't you come with me and find out?" said Mr Barn Owl.

"Yes, please," said Plop.

Mr Barn Owl blinked. "What did you say?"

"I said 'yes, please'," Plop said. "I would like to come hunting with you."

"I thought you were afraid of the dark!"

"Me?" said Plop. "Afraid of the dark! That was a *long* time ago!"

"Well!" said his father. "What are we waiting for? A-hunting we will go!"

"Hey, wait for me," said Plop's mother. "I'm coming too."

So they took off together in the moonlight, Mr and Mrs Barn Owl on each side and Plop in the middle.

Plop – the night bird.